COCKTAIL ITALIANO

COCKTAIL ITALIANO

The Definitive Guide to Aperitivo: Drinks, Nibbles, and Tales of the Italian Riviera

ANNETTE JOSEPH

Skyhorse Publishing

Skyhorse Publishing books may be purchased in bulk at special discounts for sales promotion, corporate gifts, fund-raising, or educational purposes. Special editions can also be created to specifications. For details, contact the Special Sales Department, Skyhorse Publishing, 307 West 36th Street, 11th Floor, New York, NY 10018 or info@skyhorsepublishing.com.

Skyhorse® and Skyhorse Publishing® are registered trademarks of Skyhorse Publishing, Inc.®, a Delaware corporation.

Visit our website at www.skyhorsepublishing.com.

10 9 8 7 6 5 4 3 2 1

Library of Congress Cataloging-in-Publication Data

Names: Joseph, Annette, author.
Title: Cocktail italiano: the definitive guide to aperitivo : drinks,
   nibbles, and tales of the Italian Riviera / by Annette Joseph.
Description: New York: Skyhorse Publishing, [2018] | In English. | Includes
   index.
Identifiers: LCCN 2017052517 | ISBN 9781510729971 (hardcover : alk. paper)
Subjects: LCSH: Bars (Drinking establishments)–Italy–Riviera. |
   Cocktails–Italy–Riviera. | Riviera (Italy)–Social life and customs. |
   LCGFT: Cookbooks.
Classification: LCC TX950.59.I8 J67 2018 | DDC 641.87/4094518--dc23 LC record
available at https://lccn.loc.gov/2017052517

Cover design by Janice Shay
Cover photography by Deborah Whitlaw Llewellyn

Paperback ISBN: 978-1-5107-6453-8
Hardcover ISBN: 978-1-5107-2997-1
Ebook ISBN: 978-1-5107-2999-5

Printed in China

To every drinking partner
I have ever had, and to those
in my future . . .

Cin cin xx

TABLE OF CONTENTS

HISTORY OF APERITIVO

During the eighteenth century, the ritual of enjoying cocktails before dinner became popular throughout Europe. In Italy, it caught on very quickly and remains a daily treat that most every Italian enjoys throughout the year, and especially during the summer months.

The Latin word apertus *means "to open." Torino and Milan created their own versions of drinks using bitters and vermouth, which have the effect of making one hungry, hence the name* aperitivo.

Cocktails in Italy are always paired with small bites of food that bridges the hours between lunch and a late dinner, which helps to keep one from drinking alcohol on an empty stomach. These small bites can be as simple as the uber-popular potato chip, or more layered dishes that could serve as a light supper. The recipes in this book reflect a wide array of options for parties, casual get-togethers, or just two people sharing a drink and a bite on a lazy summer afternoon. Viva Italia!

FOREWORD

by Oma Blaise Ford, *executive editor of*
Better Homes and Gardens *magazine*

The first time I went to Italy, I very predictably fell in love. My now-husband and I booked a cheap package deal to Rome with his grandmother, and we enjoyed all manner of touristy delights. We visited the Colosseum and Trevi fountain. We climbed the Spanish Steps and ate hazelnut gelato after taking in the Pantheon. We gawked upward in the Sistine Chapel and marveled at the Pietà at St. Peter's.

There was beauty and sophistication and in-real-life art history everywhere, but the love affair was really about potatoes. Thinly sliced fried potatoes, to be specific. The one truly fantastic meal we had on that trip came after a convoluted taxi ride that ended with us being dropped in a deserted-looking space between buildings and thinking perhaps we'd been set up to be robbed. When we finally recognized the understated trattoria sign and opened the door, we were immediately enveloped in warmth and good smells, whisked to a cozy table, and served a multicourse family-style dinner that required no ordering beyond choosing red or white house wine. And accompanying the meat course was a gloriously large bowl of hot homemade potato chips! Any country that legitimizes potato chips in this way must surely have my heart.

It wasn't until a number of years later on a trip with Annette that I discovered I had completely missed out on one of the best experiences Italy has to offer: *aperitivo.* I had the great good fortune to meet Annette through my work as a magazine editor and we quickly became dear and lasting friends, working and playing together. When she was renovating her first place in Liguria, she invited me along to check on the progress and get a little taste of her Italy.

1

After dragging myself through the first jet-lagged day, Annette declared that it was time for aperitivo and we strolled down the beach in Alassio, probably to Café Mozart. I don't quite remember what I drank, but I do remember the feeling of being both relaxed and energized, the civility of taking a moment at the end of the day to slow down, connect with friends, and ease toward the idea of dinner. And I remember the bowl of potato chips that accompanied that first, and nearly every subsequent, aperitivo I've enjoyed over the years.

That trip and many others with Annette cemented my love for Italy and the casual ritual of aperitivo. One of our favorite summer dinners at my house is actually a collection of aperitivo-style bites set out on the patio table and grazed upon over a leisurely couple of hours while the kids run around the yard and I sip a cocktail. We affectionately refer to it as "snacks for dinner."

There are so many things I admire about Annette, but it's her grace as a host that is perhaps most impressive. The woman knows how to throw a party and, more importantly, how to make her guests feel welcome and well taken-care of. When you arrive at Annette's house, she hands you a cocktail almost immediately and there's always a spread of delectable nibbles to which you can help yourself.

With this book, you too can tag along with Annette through the Italian Riviera and channel her effortless hospitality to recreate the aperitivo tradition in your own kitchen or backyard. Grab a friend or two, stir up an Aperol Spritz (page 54) or a Red Kiss (page 43), and don't forget those potato chips.

INTRODUCTION

Our life on the Italian Riviera started quite by accident about twenty years ago when our kids were little. A dear friend introduced us to Liguria on a family vacation, which is a region on the west coast of Italy that reminds me of the dramatic coastline of California. The landscape is similar, with steep cliffs and mountains, and the coast is dotted with colorful, picturesque seaside towns and inviting beaches.

Instead of the Tuscan vacation we initially had in mind, my husband and I rented a home in Santa Margherita, a chic Riviera town, and the rest, as they say, is history.

We soon fell in love with the daily ritual of meeting late afternoon or early evening in the main piazza or by the sea for an aperitivo. It is a ritual enjoyed up and down the Riviera, and known simply as "aperitivo," or "apero" for short. The idea of looking forward to ending the day with a cocktail and a few nibbles had me at *ciao* (hello)!

Once we settled in, aperitivo quickly became a daily habit. On the days we didn't venture into town, I would prepare a few small bites at home, and mix up an Italian apero, such as a Negroni, or Campari and soda. Even the kids enjoyed this happy break (sans alcohol, of course), because one of the basic components of an aperitivo menu is potato chips. Yes, the lowly chip has a permanent place on the apero table.

Aperitivo isn't just a beachside ritual, it's an integral part of the Italian lifestyle. Between six and eight o'clock in the evening, Italians visit a local bar to meet with friends or family, and "get the stomach prepared for dinner." At least that's the way Italians describe it. For me, it's all part of *la dolce vita*, the sweet life of Italy.

Our rental experience resulted in our buying a home on the Riviera about ten years ago. We now spend every summer there, and aperitivo is even sweeter because of the seaside location of our house and all the local friends we've made.

Aperitivo on the Italian Riviera has become my obsession—the culture, the food, the camaraderie, and of course, the cocktails. I am enamored with all the delightful variations of drinks with their interesting local and handmade ingredients, and the presentations of the many delectable plates of nibbles offered at each bar in the afternoon before the dinner hour. Especially as a recipe writer and food stylist, I became fascinated with the beautiful, yet simple local plates.

Food is an essential part of the Italian cocktail experience. With every cocktail or glass of wine or spirits one orders, a new batch of nibbles appears. Genius! Aperitivi makes for a perfect cocktail party—and we all love a party.

My husband Frank and I, along with a few friends, decided to document our apero travels throughout the Riviera over two summers. Like investigative journalists we scoured the coast, researching and photographing the best spot in every town and harbor where locals and visitors go to enjoy their apero. Rich in images of the towns, people, hotels, beaches, and bars, this book is meant to be enjoyed and experienced by all who love Italy, a party, and a cocktail, accompanied always with small plates of great food.

Peruse these pages and let me take you to all my favorite haunts, bars, and fancy drinking establishments along the coastline of this beautiful country. Each location has its own unique history, and each cocktail has its own story. I have included recipes for some of the best cocktails and food I found, so you can enjoy them at home.

This book is filled with useful and thoughtful information to introduce you to Italian cocktail culture. Read it for a virtual apero tour of the Riviera, toss it into your suitcase and go experience Italy firsthand, or create your own *Cocktail Italiano* party for your friends! It's a guidebook, a travelogue, and an Italian adventure all rolled into one tasty mouthful. Either way, I guarantee you will become an American aperophile like myself.

Live a little—no, live a lot. Enjoy *la dolce vita* and a few aperitivi from the Italian Riviera.

Italy

Liguria

Sardinia

Sicily

Genoa

Gulf of Genoa

Ligurian Sea

Loano

Alassio

Imperia

Sanremo

Bardighera

Mediterranean Sea

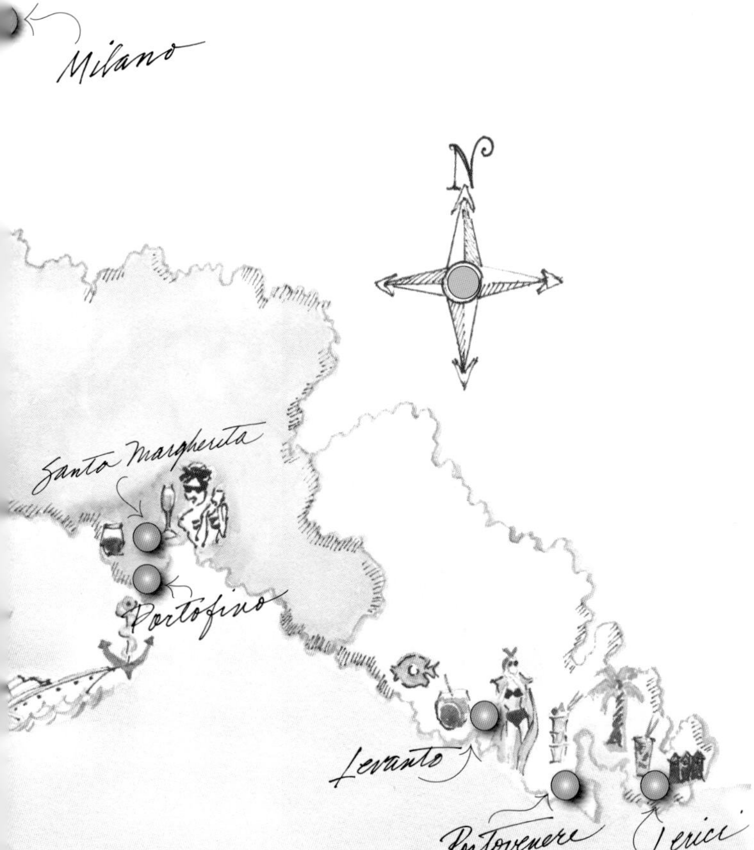

Milano

Santo Margherita

Portofino

Levanto

Portovenere

Lerici

LIGURIA

& the Italian Riviera

THE ITALIAN RIVIERA

When I first vacationed on the Italian Riviera, I was hooked by its beauty. Each seaside town is enchanting, and each one is different from the other, yet each one is a reflection of the culture and people of the Italian Riviera. Here are a few facts you'll want to know.

The Riviera is subdivided into two regions: The Riviera di Ponente, meaning "coast of the setting sun," which includes the towns from Genoa (Genova) to the French border—in this book, that includes Loano, Alassio, San Remo, Imperia, and Bordighera—and the Riviera di Levante, meaning "coast of the rising sun," including the towns of Santa Margherita, Portofino, Levanto, Lerici, and Portovenere.

From Genoa to France (from the Province of Savona to that of Imperia), in the strip of land separating Italy from the French border, lies the Riviera delle Palme (Riviera of the Palms) and the Riviera dei Fiori (Riviera of the Flowers). The Riviera delle Palme embraces the entire providence of Savona—932 square miles of coastline, mountains, and valleys where inhabitants live on the sea, and amid green pines, olive trees, and terraced vineyards.

The Riviera dei Fiori extends from Ventimiglia to Alassio and is well known for its temperate climate, and as the hub of Italy's floral business (hence the name). Most cities hold seasonal festivals, and all have boardwalks where the Riviera lifestyle is enjoyed by locals and tourists alike.

The Italian Rivera has long been the vacation destination for Italians. Italians from Turin to Milan and Genova own homes that have been in the family for generations. Families and friends enjoy yachting, swimming, sailing, and partying all summer long. They visit the same beach clubs for generations, to socialize and enjoy aperitivo at the beach clubs.

Vacationing Italians mainly visit the Riviera during the mandated vacation period called Ferragosto, an Italian holiday (though also celebrated in France) that falls on August 15th, coinciding with the Catholic Feast of the Assumption of Mary.

Not much has changed in a hundred years. The bars have been updated, but most still have a retro vibe, recalling the famous movie stars, celebrities, writers, and artists who vacationed and were inspired there in the 1950s, 60s, and 70s.

I have highlighted some of my favorite towns and favorite bars to show where to enjoy an apero or two. Salute!

BEACH CLUB MANNERS

Beach clubs dot the entire coastline of the Italian Riviera. Unlike the American understanding of a "club," the public may rent chairs, umbrellas, and cabanas for the day or by the week. Many Italian families will rent for the entire summer. The clubs are traditionally owned by Italian families, and passed down through generations. Daily fees range from 10 euros per day for a chair and an umbrella, and up to 150 euros per day at a fancy beach.

You may like to rent a cabana to change into beach clothes and store your things. This is especially helpful if you're backpacking. Most Italians go to the beach in their street clothes and change in their cabana. After a long relaxing day, they shower at the beach club and dress. If you decide to go this route, don't forget to bring toiletries! It's very civilized and very Italian.

Most beach clubs have a restaurant or bar where you can enjoy an espresso, lunch, and of course, an aperitivo at the end of a glorious summer day. Be aware that there is no wait service on the beach itself—everyone goes to the bar to order food and drinks. The dress code in club restaurants is casual, but most people throw shorts or a shirt or cover-up over their bathing suits to eat. The same goes for footwear: flip-flops are fine, but not bare feet.

So grab a lounge chair and enjoy your apero at a beach club on the Riviera. It's a great way to spend a relaxing summer day. And if you are just there for a short visit, you can still enjoy an aperitivo at the beach club bar, so don't hesitate to wander in and enjoy the sunset.

BORDIGHERA

The seaside town of Bordighera is one of the first stops on our tour of the Riviera, and a great introduction to the region. Although close to France, this town is still quintessentially Italian and offers a first sip of the Italian Riviera cocktail culture. The grand boardwalk at the seaside is wide and inviting; perfect for a morning or afternoon stroll. Brightly-colored beach clubs offer a dazzling day spent by the sea, swimming or merely whiling away hours under your bright beach umbrella. Colorful cocktails add more sparkle to the setting, and light the way to evening.

The Italian Riviera town of Bordighera is simply breathtaking. It's one of the first Italian Riviera towns you come to when driving east from the French Riviera. The distinctive tree line that frames the boardwalk, seen in the distance from the cliffs, mark the entrance to the city center (centro). Against the backdrop of the water, delicately-feathered evergreen trees along the seaside appear in relief, almost like handmade paper cutouts on a delightful pop-up card. It's no wonder that many famous painters and writers have vacationed and worked in Bordighera. Like many elegant Italian Riviera towns, European travelers flocked here in the summertime during the 1800s and early 1900s.

The abundance of formal gardens and the magnificent beauty of the beaches were a source of inspiration, along with the painterly feel of the dramatic landscape. Claude Monet was one of the many notable artists to paint the gardens of Villa Moreno in 1800s. He wrote that he was fascinated with the light. It is said (in Italy, of course) that Bordighera was where Monet's style matured.

A French influence is apparent in the art nouveau architecture seen around the town. In comparison to cities farther down the coastline, buildings here are more formal and ornate because of the nearby influence of French architecture.

Bordighera is hardly a sleepy seaside town. It is bustling with lots of chic shops and hip bars. The boardwalk along the beach is wide and full of great places to grab coffee and panini in the morning, or a proper aperitivo in the early evening.

Make sure you walk all the way down the boardwalk along the beach and stop in at one of the best bars on the coastline, La Reserve. La Reserve has a vast terrace that literally hangs over the ocean. Its breathtaking view and signature cocktails make it a must see—not to mention the owner, who has the classic looks of a movie star surfer.

The beaches are expansive at over four miles long. With a rugged stone platform on the cliffs for sunbathers to enjoy along with the many beach clubs, it has many choices for visitors to enjoy the sea. The wide beaches and easy access to public beach clubs, makes it one of the most desirable towns on the coastline. There seem to be endless striped cabanas, restaurants, and bars.

Through the middle of town runs a wide, tree-lined street named Corso Italia, an elegant location to stroll and window-shop, before sitting down in the evening for an aperitivo around 6:30 p.m. Looking up at the cliffs, be sure to take in the beautiful view of villas dotting the mountainside.

I love stopping by Buga Buga and enjoying a cocktail to music spun by a DJ, while watching the city wind down. It's the perfect stop on my way home from the beach club or a busy day scouring the flea markets across the border in France.

People enjoying aperitivo at La Reserve (see Saona Libre recipe on page 26), including the handsome owner of La Reserve at lower left.

Every beach club has its own color scheme. The beach bar kiosk on the opposite page is part of the brightly colored beach club whose colors are red and fuchsia.

Winding down the curvy roads to the city center, one sees the gorgeous pink villas that slope down to the deep blue sea.

MUSSELS IN WHITE WINE
Serves 6

Always a huge hit, mussels are offered everywhere along the Italian Riviera. Served in a huge bowl—sometimes in a giant copper pot—these steamy, buttery treats go beautifully with a cold glass of prosecco.

⅓ **cup olive oil**
1 large shallot, chopped
3 cloves garlic, chopped
2 teaspoons dried crushed red pepper
½ **teaspoon salt**
2 cups dry white wine
3½ **pounds fresh mussels, scrubbed and de-bearded**
2 tablespoons unsalted butter
½ **cup chopped fresh parsley**

Heat oil in large stockpot over medium-high heat. Add shallots, garlic, pepper, and salt, and sauté for 3 minutes until the shallots are transparent. Add the wine, bring to boil, and add mussels. Cover and cook 6 minutes, or until the shells open. Discard any mussels that do not open. Using a slotted spoon, transfer the mussels to large shallow bowl.

Boil remaining broth in the pot until liquid reduced to 1 cup. Add the butter and stir until completely incorporated. Pour the hot broth over the mussels and sprinkle with parsley.

Serve with crusty bread, and set a few big bowls around the table for the discarded shells.

COSMOPOLITAN
Serves 1

½ **ounce fresh lime juice**   1½ **ounces vodka**
1 ounce cranberry juice   **1 lime wheel**
½ **ounce Cointreau**

Add first 4 ingredients to a shaker filled with ice. Shake well and double strain into a large cocktail glass. Garnish with lime.

GRILLED VEGETABLES AND POLENTA SQUARES

Serves 6

Grilled Vegetables:
1 whole eggplant
1 whole red pepper
1 whole red onion
1 whole fennel bulb
1 whole zucchini
¼ cup olive oil
1 teaspoon salt

Polenta:
4 cups water
1 cup polenta
1 teaspoon salt
¼ cup olive oil, for grilling

Heat a grill to 400°F.

Clean and toss the whole vegetables in oil and salt. Grill on high heat for 15 minutes, turning every few minutes, until the vegetables are charred and soft. Let the grilled red pepper cool enough to peel easily under running water, then cut the pepper and the rest of the grilled vegetables into bite-sized pieces.

For the Polenta: Add the water to a medium saucepan and bring to a brisk boil over medium-high heat. Whisk the polenta into the boiling water and continue whisking until the polenta thickens.

Reduce the heat to low, cover, and continue to cook the polenta for 30 minutes, or until it has absorbed the water and thickened enough to spread.

Pour the polenta onto a 13 x 9-inch rimmed baking sheet, and use a spatula to spread it to about a ½-inch thick layer. Refrigerate for 1 hour, or until cool and firm.

Brush the heated grill lightly with olive oil.

Cut the cooled, firm polenta into 2-inch squares and brush each square with olive oil. Grill for 3 minutes, then flip the squares, brush again with olive oil, and cook another 3 minutes.

To assemble: Place the grilled polenta squares on a platter and top with the grilled vegetables.

Serve at room temperature.

FRIED CARROTS, CALAMARI, ONIONS, AND ZUCCHINI

Serves 6

8 cups water
I pound fresh calamari, or squid
2 cups all-purpose flour
I teaspoon sea salt
I teaspoon pepper
2 carrots, peeled and sliced into ¼ x 3-inch slivers
2 zucchini, sliced into ¼ x 3-inch slivers
I small red onion, peeled and sliced into ¼ x 3-inch slivers
Canola oil, for frying

Add 8 cups water to a stockpot and bring to a boil over medium-high heat. Boil the squid for I to 2 hours. The longer time will make the squid more tender. Remove and drain the squid on paper towels and pat dry.

Slice the squid into thin ¼-thick and 3-4-inch slivers.

Mix flour, salt, and pepper in a large, shallow bowl.

In a separate bowl, toss together the carrots, zucchini, and red onion.

Heat 3 inches of oil in a large cast iron pot over medium-high heat to 425°F. If you don't have a thermometer for this, add a coated vegetable to the hot oil. If it sizzles, the oil is ready.

Toss the vegetables in batches in the flour mixture—do not crowd—and use a slotted spoon to place them into the hot oil. Fry 2 to 3 minutes, until golden brown. Use a slotted spoon to transfer the vegetables to paper towels to drain.

Toss the squid pieces in the flour mixture, and fry in batches for I minute, until golden brown and crispy. Use a slotted spoon to transfer the squid to paper towels to drain.

Gently toss the vegetables and squid in a large bowl, and serve warm.

MOJITO
Serves 1

6 mint leaves, plus sprigs for garnish
2 teaspoons sugar
1 ounce fresh lime juice
1 ½ ounces white rum
½ cup crushed ice
Soda water

In a Collins glass, muddle the mint leaves with the sugar and lime juice. Add the rum and crushed ice, and top off with soda water. Garnish with sprigs of mint. Served with a straw.

SAONA LIBRE
Serves 1

This variation of a Cuba Libre calls for a traditional Italian soda, Chinotto, made from the juice of the fruit of the myrtle leaf orange tree. It has a taste that's reminiscent of Coca-Cola™. It is one of my personal favorites, and mixing it with dark rum makes for a delicious twist to a classic cocktail.

1 lime, halved
2–3 large ice cubes
2 ounces dark rum
3 ounces Chinotto, found at Italian specialty stores, and at some groceries

Squeeze the halves of lime into a Collins glass, add ice cubes, and pour in the rum. Drop in one of the spent lime shells, and fill the glass with Chinotto. Stir and enjoy!

WHITE NEGRONI

Serves 1

This variation on a classic is inspired by the addition of Suze, which is a bitter French apéritif made from the gentian root. The combination is flowery and delicious.

Crushed ice
2 ounces gin
1 ounce Lillet Blanc
¾ ounce Suze, (see Sources, page 234)
Lemon peel, for garnish

Chill a glass.

Combine all ingredients in a separate glass or cocktail shaker filled with crushed ice, and stir to chill. Strain into a chilled glass and garnish with a strip of lemon peel.

PIÑA COLADA

Serves 1

3 ounces (3 parts) pineapple juice, chilled
1 ounce (one part) white rum, chilled
1 ounce (one part) coconut cream, chilled
Pineapple wedge, for garnish
1 cup crushed ice

Chill a tall glass.

In a blender, add all ingredients except pineapple wedge, along with the crushed ice, and blend until smooth. Pour into the chilled glass, garnish with a pineapple wedge, and serve with a straw.

SAN REMO

Aperitivo is offered everywhere you go in San Remo, one of the largest cities on the Italian Riviera. I personally love to sit on the boardwalk in the early evening and enjoy an aperitivo by the sea. Of all the Riviera towns, this one has the most retro 60s Italian vibe. You almost expect Gina Lolobrigida to sit beside you at the bar. There is much to explore and enjoy in this thriving city.

When I think of San Remo I can't help but think of the beach scene in the movie *The Talented Mr. Ripley*. Rumor has is that the scenes were not actually filmed there, but I still love the idea that they were.

San Remo is a place to spend a few days exploring. The classic architecture dating from the beginning of the twentieth century and checkerboard design of the boardwalk make it distinctive and fun to explore. The boardwalk is expansive and runs for several kilometers along the shore. Surrey bikes and beach bicycles are available to rent, and a great way to see more of the city.

Unlike most Riviera towns, San Remo is not seasonal; it boasts a year-round population. If you like to gamble, San Remo has a casino which holds tournaments throughout the year. The famous San Remo Music Festival fills the town with thousands of people in February. It's one of the largest music festivals in Europe, which ensures that the wide streets of the town are also a concerto of traffic and pedestrians. Since the festival began in 1951, the most famous Italian songs are premiered here annually. It's become a beloved cultural event and the party atmosphere is something all Italians look forward to experiencing. It's certainly one of the reasons why you can find so many great bars and hotels to enjoy aperitivo.

The beaches in San Remo are some of the biggest on the Riviera, with wide expanses of sand. Seemingly endless choices of beach clubs and classy hotels line the coast. Each club has its own look, but the retro Riviera vibe is a common thread among all the clubs.

Known as the city of flowers, the city is the epicenter of the floral industry in Italy. Viewing the city from the autostrada, you will see the many greenhouses perched on the cascading terraces, as proof that most of the flowers of Italy are grown here.

San Remo is the epicenter for vintage posters depicting the Riviera life. The stylized posters are still very popular for tourists and collectors alike.

Previous page: The distinctive colorful checkered boardwalk is part of the raised boardwalk that overlooks the beach.

Opposite page, clockwise from upper left: The Aperol spritz is the preferred summertime cocktail; from the boardwalk a steep staircase leads to one of the bigger beach clubs; a Vespa parks in front of a vintage 1950's poster, a popular style seen everywhere around town; ivy grows on the lovely cottages, similar to boathouses, that line the boardwalk.

Opposite page: One of the biggest beaches on the Riviera, and bars line the streets on the port.

This page: The San Remo train station is handily located at the beach.

FRIED SARDINES

Serves 8

These salty and crunchy fried sardines are really delicious and the perfect little snack with a cocktail. We eat them with the heads on them, but of course you can remove the heads if it's not your thing.

2 pounds of fresh sardines (ask your fishmonger to gut and clean the sardines for you, and leave the heads on if you like)
1 cup all-purpose flour
1½ teaspoons sea salt, divided
3 cups olive oil

If your fishmonger hasn't done this, wash and clean the sardines, removing the insides, heads, and scales. Dry the prepared sardines with paper towels.

In a shallow bowl, mix the flour with 1 teaspoon salt, then dredge the sardines in the flour mixture.

Pour the oil in a 12-inch cast iron skillet. Attach a deep-fry thermometer to side of the skillet and heat the oil over medium-high heat until the thermometer reads 350°F, or a sardine dipped into the oil sizzles.

Fry the sardines in batches of about 6 for 2 to 3 minutes, or until golden brown, making sure they are completely immersed in the oil. Allow the oil to reheat to 350°F between batches. Remove the sardines using a slotted spoon and place on paper towels to drain. Sprinkle with the remaining ½ teaspoon salt and serve immediately.

SCAMPI POACHED IN OLIVE OIL

Serves 6 to 8

Poaching the shrimp gives them a soft consistency. It's a wonderful technique used to infuse the subtle flavor of olive oil into the shrimp.

3 cups olive oil
3 large sprigs rosemary
18 large shrimp or scampi, peeled and deveined
Salt and pepper to taste
4 lemon wedges

Add olive oil to large, heavy saucepan or skillet, and add rosemary sprigs. Attach a deep-fry thermometer to side of pan and heat the oil over medium heat until the thermometer reads between 165°F and 180°F.

Sprinkle the shrimp all over with salt and pepper, and use a slotted spoon to place the shrimp into the hot oil. Poach for 8 minutes, adjusting heat to maintain temperature between 165°F and 180°F, or just until the shrimp are opaque in the center.

Use a slotted spoon to transfer the shrimp to paper towels to drain. Serve at room temperature, and garnish with lemon wedges.

FOCACCIA SANDWICHES

Filled with Parma ham, prosciutto, cheese, or salami, these are a staple along the Italian Rivera. At almost every apero'clock they make an appearance. Use any of these ingredients that you prefer, in any amount you like (see recipe for Focaccia, page 74). These sandwiches are simple to make, yet so satisfying with a cocktail.

THE NEGRONI FIZZ
Serves 1

Cocktail aficionado and my best friend, Oma Blaise Ford, loves this twist on the Classic Negroni. According to Oma, "straight Negronis are usually too syrupy and strong for me, but that bit of sparkling rosé makes a huge difference. I use about 3 ounces of sparkling rosé per serving, which is convenient if you're making it for two and use one of those little single serving bottles. Or you could make 8 with a regular bottle of sparkling rosé."

1 ounce gin
1 ounce sweet vermouth
1 ounce Campari
2 to 3 ounces sparkling rosé wine
1 orange slice, for garnish

Using a balloon wine glass, mix the gin, vermouth, and Campari, add 3 cubes of ice, and top off with the sparkling rosé. Garnish with an orange slice and serve.

PANZANELLA (BREAD SALAD WITH MINT)
Serves 4

3 cups of stale bread, cut into 1-inch cubes
6 tablespoons olive oil, divided
1 teaspoon salt, divided
2 tablespoons balsamic vinegar
1 cup baby tomatoes, cut into halves
¼ red onion, thinly sliced
½ cup mint leaves, chiffonade
3 tablespoons capers

Preheat the oven to 350°F.

In a large bowl, toss the bread with 3 tablespoons olive oil, add ½ teaspoon salt, and toss to distribute. Place the bread cubes on a cookie sheet and toast them for 10 minutes, or until golden.

In a large serving bowl, whisk together the remaining 3 tablespoons oil and the vinegar. Add the toasted bread, tomatoes, onion, mint, capers, and remaining salt, and toss to combine. Set aside at room temperature for at least 1 hour to allow the flavors to combine before serving. Serve in small individual bowls.

RED KISS

Serves 1

Fernet-Branca is one of my favorite Italian Amaro. Amaro is a syrupy digestive liqueur specific to Italy. There are a number of regional versions infused with local herbs and spices. You will always find an amazing selection of Amaro on a side table at your favorite local restaurant on the Riviera. Fernet has an acquired bitter taste, much like espresso or Campari, but it's something that warms the stomach and it is as unique as it is delicious. I enjoy sipping it after dinner with a lone ice cube, but I find that adding it to a mixed drink, such as this one, makes a savory and interesting cocktail. (Read more about Amaros on page 44.)

2 ounces Campari
¼ ounce Cynar (an artichoke-infused liqueur)
¼ ounce Fernet-Branca

1 ounce white vermouth
15 drops orange bitters
3 orange twists

Fill a cocktail shaker with ice, and add the Campari, Cynar, Fernet, vermouth, and bitters. Stir until well-chilled, and strain into a highball glass. Squeeze 2 orange peels to release essential oil into the cocktail, and garnish with the remaining orange peel.

HERB MARINATED OLIVES

Serves 8

¼ cup olive oil
4 cups mixed olives
3 whole cloves garlic, smashed
2 teaspoons red pepper flakes

3 tablespoons chopped fresh rosemary
2 tablespoons chopped fresh marjoram
1 tablespoon fresh thyme leaves

In a sauté pan over medium heat, add the oil and warm the olives, garlic, and pepper flakes for 3 minutes. Add the herbs to the olive mixture and toss for 1 minute. Remove from the heat and serve warm.

MORE ABOUT AMARO

Amaro means "bitter." Italians love a taste of bitter, hence the popularity of the Negroni and the Campari soda. It's becoming popular in the States, but in Italy it is already a staple and has been since the inception of the digestive (which consequently led to the aperitivo, and the now very popular aperitivo ritual).

Amaro (bitters) are Italian herbal liqueurs, and each Italian family has their own unique, secret recipe that can include as few as four or more than thirty ingredients, such as herbs, roots, artichokes, fennel, citrus peels, and spices. All resulting amari share a bitter-sweet quality. I am friends with the family that produces China Clementi, and I assure you the family recipe is well-guarded.

It's commonly enjoyed as a digestivo in Italy since it is in the bitter family—it's an acquired taste that is becoming more popular with cocktail enthusiasts. In Italy, amari are typically consumed while standing at a bar, or after dinner when a bottle of the house's preferred amaro is set on the table once the plates are cleared. Some brands, like Fernet-Branca, Ramazzotti, and Averna, have even become national names in Italy, available at bars and trattorias up and down the Italian peninsula. One of the most popular amaros is Fernet, and in some spots it's even served on tap.

Most recently, amari are being used in modern cocktail recipes, such as the Red Kiss. Here are 11 of the most popular Amari: Fernet-Branca, Cio Ciaro Amaro, Amaro Nonino Quintessentia, Cynar 70 Proof Amaro, Amaro Montenegro, Varnelli Amaro Dell'Erborista, Amaro Lucano, Cardamaro Amaro, Averna Amaro Liqueur, Braulio Amaro, China Clementi (pronounced ki-na).

Federica and her family are fourth-generation creators of China Clementi, an amaro available in the family pharmacy in Fivizzano near Lerici, and all over Italy.

WHISKEY SOUR

Serves 1

1 ½ ounces whiskey, or Bourbon
1 ounce lemon juice
1 cherry
Lime wedge
Simple Syrup:
1 cup sugar
1 cup water

Place all ingredients into a cocktail shaker filled with ice cubes. Shake then strain into a highball glass filled with fresh ice. Garnish with a cherry and lime wedge.

To make simple syrup: Combine 1 cup sugar and 1 cup water in a saucepan over medium-high heat. Bring to a boil, stir, and immediately set aside to cool. Simple syrup can be used in a number of cocktail recipes, so it is good to have on hand. It will keep, refrigerated, up to 2 months.

KON TIKI

Serves 1

2 ounces Scotch whiskey
1 ounce dark rum
1 ounce Cointreau orange liqueur

Fill a cocktail shaker with ice, add all ingredients, and shake to chill. Strain into a chilled martini glass.

IMPERIA

I discovered this town through my friend Forrest. He asked me along to meet some artist friends for drinks here one day, and the charm of the industrial setting was not lost on me. It's become a regular cocktail destination. Near the working marina, the pink portico and retro bars captivated me immediately. Imperia is a little rough around the edges, but the lack of polish makes it authentically Italian, and gives it a very working-class feel, which endears it to me.

Imperia is the capital of the Provence of Imperia. Mussolini created the city in 1923 to be the capital of Liguria, hence the autocratic name. In truth, although the town was founded to be the seat of Liguria, it never became that. Instead, it remains a pretty little Riviera town with quaint narrow streets, a rather industrial boardwalk, and a pink portico on the old marina at the edge of town, named Portici della banchina di Oneglia.

The old marina mainly docks fishing boats and, every once in a while, a yacht or two. The setting provides a very hip urban backdrop to the city. Just steps from the marina, one can have an aperitivo or two under a striking pink portico. Sitting here is decidedly pleasant, enjoying the vintage shop and restaurant signs—very post WWII, very old school. There's one retro bar I cannot get enough of: Bar La Conchiglia. The art deco shell décor is spectacular, and the swoon-worthy, stripey chairs make me want to move right in.

The Museum of Olive Oil is located there and like San Remo, Imperia also has a huge flower industry. Imperia is very Italian in the sense that a large population lives there all year-round and in the summer, and it is an Italian tourist destination.

The distinctive pink walls and porticos line the port.

Imperia is a great stop on your way down the coast—the seafood is sublime and you will feel like you're in an undiscovered gem. I like to visit just to see what's new, and to lunch at old favorites like Braceria Matama. I suggest you make a stop mid-day for coffee or an aperitif at Canna Ramella. It is a super shop that sells kitchen wares and gifts, with a magical little bar and a lovely bartendress. Aperitivo crowds are smaller here, with many locals in attendance, and the overall feel is more casual.

There's something really groovy about Imperia that makes me want to come back again and again.

Friendly baristas and surfers alike enjoy cocktails along this pink port. The drink on lower left is an Americano.

ORANGE MARINATED FENNEL WITH PECORINO SHAVINGS

Serves 4

You can make this in the morning and let sit out all day to marinate.

¼ cup apple balsamic vinegar (I prefer Ritrovo brand, or
  substitute apple cider vinegar.)
½ cup orange juice
½ teaspoon salt
2 tablespoons olive oil
4 oranges, peeled and sliced into ¼-inch thick rounds
I large fennel bulb, sliced paper-thin
½ cup small black olives
I cup shaved Pecorino cheese

Combine the vinegar, orange juice, salt, and oil in a bowl.

Place the orange and the fennel slices on a serving platter and
pour the vinegar mixture over them. Sprinkle the olives over the
oranges and fennel. Finish with sprinkles of the cheese. Serve with
small plates and forks for each person.

APEROL SPRITZ

Serves I

2 ounces Aperol
3 ounces prosecco
I ounce soda
I orange slice

Fill a large wine glass with ice and add the Aperol, Prosecco, and
finish off with the soda.

Garnish with a slice of orange.

SEARED TUNA WITH OLIVE SAUCE

Serves 6

Olive Sauce:
½ **cup fresh parsley**
½ **cup fresh basil**
⅓ **cup chopped imported green olives, pitted, or Taggiasca olives (see Sources, page 234)**
1 **small clove garlic, minced**
2 **tablespoons lemon juice**
3 **teaspoons extra-virgin olive oil**
⅛ **teaspoon salt**

1 **pound ahi tuna, trimmed and cut into 1½-inch steak**
1 **tablespoon extra-virgin olive oil**
¼ **teaspoon salt**
⅛ **teaspoon freshly ground pepper**

To prepare the olive sauce: Combine the parsley, basil, olives, garlic, lemon juice, oil, and salt in the bowl of a food processor and pulse until smooth.

Preheat a grill to medium-high.

Rub the tuna steak overall with oil and season with salt and pepper. Place the tuna on the grill and sear 2 to 3 minutes, then turn and sear another 2 to 3 minutes. The tuna should be seared, but pink inside when done.

Thinly slice the tuna into 12 bite-sized pieces, transfer to a serving plate, and drizzle with olive sauce. Serve warm, or at room temperature. Pass around the table or serve on separate small plates for individual servings.

GIN FIZZ

Serves 1

All along the Riviera, old-school cocktails have enjoyed a resurgence of popularity. One of my personal favorites is a Gin Fizz; I love the sweet and sour notes. It is refreshingly cool, and quenches your thirst after a day at the beach.

3 ounces gin
1 ounce fresh lemon juice
1 tablespoon powdered sugar

3 ounces club soda
1 thin lemon slice, for garnish

In a cocktail shaker filled with ice, add gin, lemon juice, and powdered sugar; shake to combine. Strain into a glass filled with ice. Top it off with the club soda, and garnish with a lemon slice.

STUFFED SARDINES
Serves 8

Although the Italian Riviera spans the coastline of the Liguria Sea, most of the sea life has been fished to the point that only small fish can be found. Not to worry! Ligurians are very good at making use of what they have, and making the most of it. Tiny fish appear on every menu and there are many different and tasty preparations. Stuffed Sardines are one of my favorite dishes and serving these for aperitivo is a great addition to the table.

16 fresh sardines, scaled, cleaned, and gutted (ask your fishmonger to do this for you, or see below for instructions on gutting)
2 cups fresh breadcrumbs
1 cup flat-leaf parsley leaves
½ cup freshly grated Parmesan cheese
1 egg, beaten
½ teaspoon salt
¼ cup olive oil + 2 tablespoons
Lemon for garnish

To gut the sardines, remove the head and innards of each sardine (you can do this in one action by pulling the head downwards; the innards should come, too). Run your thumb from the cavity down to the tail, using a knife to butterfly the sardines. Press them flat.

In the bowl of a food processor, add the breadcrumbs, parsley, Parmesan, egg, and salt, and pulse until combined.

Place a sardine skin-side down in the palm of your hand, and put a tablespoon of breadcrumb stuffing in the cavity of the fish. Gently press together so the crumb mixture will adhere to the fish, and be very careful when you flip them over in the pan.

Heat ¼ cup oil in a frying pan over medium-high heat until a sardine placed in the oil sizzles. Fry the sardines 4 at a time, filling-side down, for 3 minutes, so that the filling stays inside the fish. Then carefully turn and fry 3 minutes on the other side, until golden.

Carefully transfer the sardines to a serving platter. Sprinkle with 2 tablespoons olive oil, and garnish with lemon wedges. Serve warm.

EGGPLANT CAMPONATA WITH CROSTINI
Serves 8

This has been my favorite tried-and-true apero recipe for many years. I make a lot and I keep it in the fridge for unexpected guests. It's also an amazing topping for pizza, another great aperitivo snack.

¼ **cup olive oil**
1 small red onion, finely chopped
4 cloves garlic, crushed or coarsely chopped
4 cups cubed eggplant (about 1 large eggplant), skin-on, cut in 1-inch cubes
1 cup chopped tomatoes
1 cup chopped fresh basil
¼ **cup capers**
½ **cup balsamic vinegar**
½ **cup tomato sauce (store-bought is fine, unless you have homemade)**
1 teaspoon red pepper flakes
Salt and pepper to taste
Parmesan cheese, for garnish
Crostini (recipe on page 72)

Add the oil to a large pan over medium heat, and sauté the chopped onions and garlic for 3 to 5 minutes, until translucent. Add all remaining ingredients, except the Parmesan cheese. Decrease the heat to low, cover, and stir frequently (so the camponata does not stick) for 30 to 40 minutes, until the eggplant and tomatoes are combined and softened.

Spread onto sliced crostini, served warm, or at room temperature, or even cold—it's all good (but be sure to sprinkle with Parmesan). This will keep in a sealed container, refrigerated, for up to 2 weeks.

BEER AMERICANO

Serves 1

This cocktail has become very popular all along the Riviera, among Italians and tourists alike. Substituting beer for the soda makes this a very refreshing summer choice. It was created in Milan for the opening of the Trussardi Flagship Store by resident bartender Tommaso Cecca. Perfect for a sweltering summer evening. You'll love it!

1½ ounces Campari
1½ ounces sweet vermouth
3 ounces lager beer, your choice brand
Lemon zest, for garnish

Combine the Campari, vermouth, and several ice cubes in a tall tumbler, and stir to combine.

Pour the beer into another glass, and stir to create a stiff foam. Remove the foam with a spoon, and top the cocktail with about 3 ounces of the beer foam. Garnish with lemon zest.

Note: For a lighter Americano, feel free to stir 2 ounces of the beer into the cocktail as well. However, this should be done before you top the cocktail with the foam.

ALASSIO

Alassio is defined by endless beach clubs, chic shopping, and trendy restaurants. For families from Milan and Turin, it is the popular place to summer, mainly because it offers an array of summer fun and boasts one of the largest sandy beaches on the Riviera. And it doesn't hurt that perfect aperitivo awaits you around every corner.

According to the legend, the name of the town came from Adelasia, the daughter of Ottone I of Saxony who was emperor of the Sacred Roman Empire from 936 to 972. She was said to be in love with Aleramo, a young cup-bearer at court (no, he wasn't serving apero!), and that the emperor was not at all happy about the love affair. The two lovers escaped to the misty regions of Germany, where, after being married and surviving many ups and downs, they came to settle at the foot of Mount Tirasso.

The place where Adelasia and Aleramo settled became the town Alaxia, now known as Alassio, so the story goes.

What is known for sure is that Alassio became a tourist resort in the late nineteenth century, thanks to the large presence of the British. The Hanburys greatly contributed to Alassio's development with the creation of gardens on the hills and the construction of some typically English buildings. The Italian Riviera has always been a playground for the British; many towns still have a few English pubs. In Alassio, there are three English pubs, and an English tennis club.

Alassio has a beautiful seaside boardwalk shaded by tall palms that runs along the beach for more than 3 kilometers, always within sight of the blue bay that embraces Alassio and Laigueglia. Alassio is also known to have the longest sandy beach in Italy.

The "Budello," as it's known, is a pedestrian-only main street that runs through downtown. Shopping and strolling here is a favorite activity for locals and vacationers, and, of course, stopping for an aperitivo is a daily ritual not to be missed.

Another pleasant walk, called "The Winter Promenade," starts at the Spanish bastion at the eastern end of the city and heads to the Yachting Port, just beside the tiny Chapel by the Sea. Sandon's Yacht Club near the marina is a good place to pause for a cocktail along the way.

Keep in mind that Alassio has long been a favorite watering hole of writers and celebrities, such as Lord Byron, Ernest Hemingway, and Charlie Chaplin. In fact, the original bar they all visited for aperitivo is still there—the award-winning Café Roma in town.

Across from Café Roma, the Muretto is a local attraction. The Muretto's low, tiled walls feature hand-painted tiles by artists and writers. It is said that Charlie Chaplin and Ernest Hemingway came up with this decorating idea.

Café Mozart is on the boardwalk and is owned by the same people as Café Roma. It is a classical setting, right on the sea, and the trompe l'oeil (a French word meaning, "trick of the eye") painting on the walls inside are breathtaking, so don't miss them.

Don't forget to head to the hills for a visit to Villa Della Pergola, a boutique hotel that affords a breathtaking vista of Alassio while you sip their special version of Aperol Spritz.

Alassio was my home for more than twelve years. It's the place I first fell deeply in love with the Italian Rivera and the apero lifestyle. Needless to say, I have spent endless evenings enjoying cocktails and nibbles at Café Roma and Café Mozart.

Clockwise from upper left: Vintage beach graphics are seen all over town; colorful buildings line the seaside; colorful cabanas like this one are for hire at each beach club; a child runs past the mosaic tile medallion on the new pier.

CREPES

CAF...ERIA

CREPES SALATE

COCKTAILS

Both public and private beaches are available for a fun day of sun. The incredible colors don't stop at the shoreline.

CAFÉ ROMA

Ernest Hemingway's favorite bar on the Italian Riviera, Café Roma, is one of the oldest bars in Alassio and is still a place to go for an aperitivo. The story goes that Hemingway felt so at home at the bar that he left his parrot there for safe-keeping while he traveled the Riviera. The current owners are Massimo and his beautiful wife, Lucia; they also own Café Mozart on the boardwalk.

This page: The stunning interior at Café Mozart. Opposite page: From simple to sophisticated, there are many choices of beach and town bars to enjoy an aperitivo.

TOMATO BRUSCHETTA
Serves 12

Bruschetta is an antipasta (starter dish) using grilled bread slices topped with olive oil and salt. Variations on toppings include grilled vegetables, tomatoes, beans, cured meat, and/or cheese. Ripe summer tomatoes in Italy are incredibly sweet and juicy. I love to drain the tomatoes into a bowl and reserve the tomato juices. Don't mash the tomatoes, but gently press them to drain off the juice. Note: the tomato juice makes a delicious addition to any savory cocktail, including your favorite Bloody Mary recipe.

Tomato Topping:
6 ripe Roma tomatoes, diced and drained into a bowl
   (refrigerate and reserve the juice for cocktails)
3 tablespoons olive oil
6 basil leaves, chopped
2 cloves garlic, minced
½ teaspoon salt
½ teaspoon pepper

Toss all ingredients in a separate bowl. Set aside at room temperature while you make the crostini (toasted bread slices).

To make the Crostini:
1 baguette, cut into ½-inch thick slices
½ cup of olive oil

Preheat the oven to 375°F.

In a large bowl, toss the bread slices with the olive oil.

Place the oiled slices on a baking sheet, and bake for 10 minutes, or until golden brown.

To assemble: Place 2 tablespoons of the tomato topping on each toast slice, and serve at room temperature.

FOCACCIA

Serves 4

One of my first stops in this little beach town is to a focacceria, which is a bakery in this region of Italy that usually specializes in focaccia bread. When our guests arrive every summer, I take great pleasure in introducing them to the local focaccia, called "focaccia di recco." What's the big deal, you ask? Something about the water and the flour, the salt, and sea air in Alassio rocks the focaccia. This version is delicious and close to the original, but—full disclosure—it's never quite the same as eating the Alassio version. Some things defy perfect replication.

1 package dry yeast
⅓ cup warm water + more as needed
**3 cups double zero flour, or super fine bread flour (I like
    Antimo Caputo from Antico Mulino Napoli brand)**
**½ cup extra-virgin olive oil + 1 teaspoon for the cookie
    sheet + 4 tablespoons**
2 tablespoons coarse salt + 1 teaspoon for finishing

Preheat the oven to 450°F.

In the bowl of a standing mixer fitted with a dough hook, place the yeast in the bowl, stir in ⅓ cup warm water, and wait 10 minutes until bubbles have formed. At this point, the yeast is proofed. Add the flour, ½ cup oil, and 2 tablespoons salt, and beat until it forms a very sticky dough. Add more water as needed if the dough seems dry.

Flour a work surface and turn the dough onto floured surface. Knead gently for a minute until the dough comes together to form a ball. Be careful not to overknead; the dough should remain soft. Oil a 10 x 14-inch cookie sheet with a lip. **Note:** you can use parchment paper to line the cookie sheet but I like to oil the paper.

Spread the dough out to fit the cookie sheet using your hands or a rolling pin. Using your index fingers, poke dimples into just the top of the dough. Let it rise for 30 minutes at room temperature, then again poke dimples into the risen dough, and let it rest for another 30 minutes.

Before placing the dough in the oven, drizzle with 3 tablespoons olive oil and sprinkle with 1 teaspoon coarse salt.

Bake at 450°F for 30 minutes. Remove and sprinkle with 1 more tablespoon olive oil. Let the focaccia cool slightly, slice, and eat warm or at room temperature. The key is to let the oil soak in as the focaccia cools. Leftover bread can be sealed and stored at room temperature up to 3 days.

Serving Tip: I love to use focaccia as an appetizer with olive spread, Parmesan cheese, Parma ham, and a crisp summer rosé wine. This makes the perfect start to a perfect evening.

SPICY ORANGE SHRIMP
Serves 6

Seaside nibbles always include a shrimp dish. I love the bright and spicy flavor combination of orange, mint, and hot pepper reduction. It's great to peel and enjoy shrimp with a cocktail. Tip: Make sure you have plenty of napkins and wet wipes on hand.

2 pounds whole shrimp, shells on
3 tablespoons olive oil
I shallot, chopped
I teaspoon fresh thyme
I teaspoon fresh basil
I teaspoon fresh mint
2 cups fresh orange juice
I teaspoon sea salt
I teaspoon hot pepper flakes

Rinse the shrimp in their shells with cold water and place in a strainer to drain.

In a large, 12-inch sauté pan over medium heat, stir the oil and shallots for 4 minutes, until translucent. Stir in the herbs, orange juice, salt, and hot pepper flakes, and increase the heat to high. Bring to a boil, then reduce the heat to medium, add the shrimp, and cook 8 to 10 minutes, stirring often, until the shrimp turn bright orange. Use a slotted spoon to remove the shrimp and transfer to a serving bowl. Continue to cook the sauce until is has reduced by half.

Pour the sauce over the shrimp and serve warm, or at room temperature.

PIZZA WITH BOTTARGA, RICOTTA, AND TOMATO, FROM LA LANTERNA

Serves 6 to 8

This easy pizza is perfect to enjoy with aperitvo on a hot summer night. Bottarga is a southern specialty in Italy—the roe of gray mullet or tuna that has been salted, pressed, and air-dried. The combination of the sweet tomatoes, the salty bottarga, and the smooth, creamy finish of the ricotta is wonderful. This recipe is from the best pizzeria in Alassio, La Lanterna, a restaurant on the beach and the liveliest place to enjoy the sunset. Of course, It doesn't hurt that the owner, Matteo, is very handsome and the quintessential charming Italian host.

Pizza Crust:
- 2 packages dried fast acting yeast
- 1 cup warm water
- 6 cups flour (option: you can also use 4 cups white flour and 2 cups wheat flour)
- 1 cup olive oil + 1 teaspoon for drizzling
- 2 teaspoons salt

Topping:
- 4 tablespoons ricotta cheese
- 4 slices tomato (1 large tomato), or ½ cup small tomatoes, halved
- ½ cup grated bottarga (see Sources, page 234)
- ¼ cup micro greens

In the bowl of a stand mixer fitted with a dough hook, place the yeast and ⅓ cup warm water, and wait 10 minutes until bubbles have formed. Add the flour, cup of oil, salt, and beat until it forms a very sticky dough. Add more water as needed if the dough seems dry.

Oil a large bowl, add the dough, and knead until it holds together to form a large ball. Cover the bowl tightly with plastic wrap and let sit for at least 1 hour to rise. After an hour, punch down the dough, re-seal with plastic wrap, and allow the dough to rise for 1 more hour.

Preheat oven to 450°F. Use your hands or a rolling pin to spread the dough onto a pizza pan, and drizzle the dough with 1 teaspoon olive oil. Bake for 10 to 15 minutes until golden brown. While the crust is still warm, spread the ricotta over the crust, and sprinkle with the tomatoes, grated bottarga, and micro greens. Serve warm.

RAW OYSTERS WITH LEMON SLICES
Serves 4

You can't live in an Italian beach town without enjoying raw oysters, so if you like them, don't be afraid of serving them at home. Make sure the oysters you choose to serve are tightly closed. Rinse them thoroughly with cold water. The tricky part is shucking, so please be careful and have the right tools on hand.

To have on hand:
1 hand towel, or glove for holding the oyster
1 oyster-shucking knife
1 cutting board
12 oysters (3 each)
2 or 3 lemons, sliced into wedges

Hold the shucking knife curved-side down on a cutting board. Wrap the oyster in a kitchen towel and hold it in one hand as you use the other hand to pry open the shell using the tip of the knife. Take your time and gently wiggle the shell open with the knife. Once it's open, discard the top shell and then cut around the oyster to loosen the meat. Keep each oyster in its shell and arrange on a platter of ice with lots of lemon wedges. Serve ice cold.

AMERICANO
Serves 1

Ironically, as classic Italian Cocktails go, this one is as classic as it gets. This cocktail is a perfect balance of bitter Campari liqueur and sweet Vermouth.

1½ ounces Campari
1½ ounces Italian vermouth
Splash of soda
1 twist lemon

Fill a highball glass with ice, pour in all ingredients, and garnish with a twist of lemon.

CLASSIC NEGRONI
Serves 1

Another classic Italian cocktail, the Negroni has become very popular in America in the last five years. Be aware, this is a very strong cocktail.

1 ounce dry gin
1 ounce Campari
1 ounce Italian vermouth
Cracked ice
1 twist orange peel

Add the gin, Campari, and vermouth to a cocktail shaker filled with cracked ice and shake well. Strain into a chilled highball glass with a couple of ice cubes, and garnish with a twist of orange peel.

WHAT IS VERMOUTH?

Vermouth is a key ingredient in many aperitivo cocktails, but what is it exactly?

Vermouth is fortified wine, Meaning a wine that's been distilled for a higher alcohol content. Vermouth is distilled along with botanicals, such as spices, herbs, and seeds, and then spiked with brandy. Exactly what herbs and spices remains a company secret with most manufacturers.

Martini vermouth became popular in the 1930s as a digestive. It became a social ritual to drink vermouth, served in tiny cordial glasses with a twist of lemon, to "open the stomach" before dinner. The sweet versions of vermouth were quite popular, but dry vermouth was used in many cocktails, or just sweetened with sugar.

When American cocktails became popular in Italy in the 1960s, along with the films of James Bond, the Martini Cocktail was everyone's favorite drink ... and the essential ingredient was a splash of dry vermouth.

With the Negroni taking a front seat on cocktail lists at many prestigious bars, vermouth has enjoyed a resurgence over the last decade, and no longer sits at the back of the bar gathering dust. It's true that everything old becomes new again.

YELLOW BIRD

Serves 4

Like most Americans, Italians enjoy fruity drinks in hot weather, too. Every seaside bar offers specialty cocktails all summer long, and this is a favorite.

1 cup **light rum**
½ cup **Creme de Banana**
¼ cup **Tia Maria**
3 cups **orange juice**
¼ cup **pineapple juice**

Fill a pitcher with ice. Stir all ingredients together, then pour into chilled hurricane glasses, garnish with summer fruit slices if you like, and serve.

VIRGIN STRAWBERRY DAIQUIRI

Serves 4

In Italy, apero is a family affair, which means children are included in aperitivo. There are lots of juices and virgin cocktails available to mix up a great non-alcoholic treat. Plus those potato chips and little nibbles before dinner are a big hit with the younger crowd.

Note: For an adult version, add 1 ounce of rum to the mixture.

1 cup **crushed ice**
¼ cup **frozen strawberries**
1 ounce **lime juice**
2 tablespoons **sugar**

Place the ice, strawberries, lime juice, and sugar in a blender, and blend until it's the consistency of a smoothie. Serve with straws.

The Italians allow children to enjoy a non~alcohol aperitivo, and menus offer many choices of virgin cocktails.

VILLA DELLA PERGOLA APEROL SPRITZ

Serves 1

Named one of Condé Nast Traveler's top 50 hotels, the Villa Della Pergola will take your breath away it's so lovely. Perched high on a cliff overlooking the entire town of Alassio and the sea, it's a quintessentially Italian hotel, known also for impeccable service. Like many hotels in Italy this location was once a privately-owned villa. The extravagant gardens are amazing, and tours are conducted on Sundays—a perfect time to enjoy the gardens, then sit on the terrace and enjoy the view and a signature cocktail, their own version of the Aperol Spritz.

Lemon sugar, for the rim (see Sources, page 234)
½ cup lemonade (recipe below)
½ cup Aperol
Splash prosecco
¼ orange slice, for garnish

Fill a shallow saucer with lemon sugar.

Rub the rim of a white wine glass with water and dip into the lemon sugar to coat.

Fill the glass half full with ice and add the lemonade, then add the Aperol, top off the glass with the Prosecco, garnish with an orange wedge, and serve with a straw.

Lemonade

Serves 8

This is how to make fresh lemonade, but you can also substitute store-bought in a pinch. I like the Italian brand from San Pellegrino.

1½ cups lemon juice (4 to 5 lemons)
1¾ cups sugar
8 cups of water

Stir together all ingredients in a pitcher until sugar dissolves, and refrigerate until needed.

If you have leftover lemonade, just cover and refrigerate up to 2 days.

LOANO

This classic Italian town is not on most tourists' must-see radar. But the insider scoop is that the state of the art marina and yacht club has the most beautiful bar on the Riviera. Stop in and lounge with the locals—you'll be happy you did.

Loano used to be a sleepy beach town, not particularly scenic or hip—a town mainly visited by Italian families who have been going to the beach club all their lives. In other words, Loano is a strictly Italian destination. That is, until about five years ago.

That was when Loano made the brillaint decision to build a state of the art marina, Yacht Club Marina Di Loano. The Yacht Club has restaurants and a chic hotel. It's one of the most modern and beautiful locations I have had the pleasure of visiting for aperitivo on the Riviera—definitely worth the stop.

I adore going there with friends and watching the sunset from the wrap-around terrace at Yacht Club Marina di Loana. The restaurant has first class service and an amazing local menu, plus the owner (and sometimes bartender) is a hoot.

I was happy to discover it a few years ago, thanks to friends, and it's now on my must-do list every summer.

Opposite: The gigantic brand new modern yacht club overlooks the marina, one of the largest on the Riviera, and a great place to dock your boat.

Pages 90~91: A rooftop bar and restaurant is located on the top floor of the yacht club. The expansive view is worth the trip to the city.

SCAMPI WITH LEMON

Serves 8

6 cups ice in a bowl
4 pounds large shrimp, shell on
2 lemons, cut into wedges

Fill a large stockpot half full of water and bring to a boil over high heat.

Fill a large bowl with 6 cups ice.

Drop the shrimp in the boiling water and cook 3 minutes, until the shrimp turn red. Drain the shrimp and immediately submerge them in the bowl of ice.

Arrange the shrimp and lemon wedges decoratively on a platter, or atop a separate ice-filled bowl to keep them chilled, and serve.

VODKA WITH CUCUMBER
Serves 1

2 ounces cucumber vodka
1 ounce tonic
½ ounce fresh lime juice
1 or 2 cucumber slices, for garnish
1 sprig fresh mint, for garnish

Fill a highball glass with ice, then add the cucumber vodka, tonic, and lime juice, and stir. Garnish with the cucumber slices, and a sprig of mint.

WATERMELON DAIQUIRI
Serves 2

Sometimes it's fun to have an over-dressed cocktail. The bartender at the yacht club in Loano loves to garnish his specialty drinks—flowers, watermelon wedges, anything goes. This Watermelon Daiquiri is no exception.

2 cups chopped watermelon
1 tablespoon lime zest
6 ounces light rum
1 teaspoon powdered sugar
1 ounce lime juice
2 small slices watermelon, with rind

Puree the watermelon and the lime zest in a food processor, then strain into a small bowl.

Pour the strained puree into a large ice-filled cocktail shaker and add the rum, sugar, and lime juice. Cover, shake, and strain into 2 small tumblers. Garnish with watermelon slices.

GENOVA

With its historical center, bustling street life, and working port, Genova is the best kept secret in Italy and one of my favorite destinations. If you stay long enough, you will discover the magical portocelli that can be found all along the bay. Portocelli are tiny fishing ports that are always great aperitivo hangouts. The local fishermen and shopkeepers stop by after work and enjoy a cocktail or glass of wine before heading home. It's fun to see elegant patrons in suits standing on the sand enjoying their daily ritual of apero.

One of the prettiest and busiest of these ports is called Boccadasse. Its pretty, brightly-painted buildings reach down to a breathtaking bay—it's the perfect place to enjoy a cocktail and watch the sunset.

Our introduction to Genova was about twenty years ago. My husband and I were staying in Santa Margherita, and wanted to take our small children to visit an aquarium. The closest big city with an aquarium was Genova. It is the capital of Liguria, and—though we didn't realize it at the time—also one of the capitals of industry in Italy. We piled into the car and traveled forty-five minutes up the coast from our summer rental until we found ourselves in the center of this industrial port town, hopelessly lost. Finally we found the aquarium, situated on the port between container ships the size of skyscrapers.

Our friends Forrest and Roberto live in a swanky postwar flat on the port side of the city, with amazing views of the docked ships in the harbor. They look like sculptures that are part of the living room decor. Over the past decade, Forrest introduced me to his city with walking tours and, of course, many stops for aperitivo. He is my partner in crime and drinking, and we have done our share of hanging out and eating in a variety of bars across the city.

Being an important port, Genova is known for its international food flavor profiles, based on spices imported from all over the world. It would be worthwhile to take a food tour when you visit. However, aperitivo retains a distinct Italian flavor all around the city, even though the cuisine reflects an international flare. Genova holds firmly to its Italian heritage when it comes to the tradition of apero. The magical aperitivo hour offers myriad choices, from small family-owned bars with signature drinks like Cavo-Marescotto, to the classic locals' bar like Bar Mangini in the heart of Genova.

The old center of the city flaunts wide walking streets and beautiful architecture with unique trompe l'oeil embellishments on many buildings. You can get lost in the maze of tiny streets and wind up on a beautiful piazza with grand fountains and towering buildings embellished with stone patterns—distinctly Genovese.

Genova is a city that's overlooked by most American tourists, but should definitely be included on your travel agenda. It's an Italian Riviera treasure and a great place to take an apero and spend some relaxing hours simply people-watching.

The Bogadasse port is a fisherman's port where everyone congregates for aperitivo and to watch the sunset.

ROBERTO'S RAW BABY ARTICHOKE SALAD WITH LEMON AND PARMESAN

Serves 8

I had never eaten a raw artichoke until about twelve years ago—and, of course, it was in Italy.

We were visiting our best friends in Genova, Forrest and Roberto, chatting away in the kitchen, when Roberto (who's actually an Italian prince from the region of Savona on the Riviera) grabbed a few baby artichokes, and began running them under cold water. He patted them dry and quickly ran them through a mandolin, slicing them paper-thin. He put them in a bowl, and proceeded to douse them in Ligurian olive oil, added salt and a flourish of lemon juice, and finished it all off with shaved Parmesan. While Forrest poured a lovely chilled Vermentino, we snacked on raw artichokes and sipped vino. For me, this was a whole new way of enjoying artichokes.

Tip: make sure that the artichokes are very fresh and tender.

2 pounds (about 20) tender baby artichokes (you may substitute the interior soft leaves and heart of larger artichokes, but do not use the tough outer leaves.)

2 lemons, halved

4 tablespoons extra-virgin olive oil

1 to 1½ teaspoons salt

2 ounces Parmesan

Trim away any tough outer leaves of the artichokes to expose their tender pale green interior. Using a knife with a serrated blade, cut off the spiky top ⅓ of the artichokes. (**Note:** baby artichokes will not have the spikes.) Use a vegetable peeler to remove the tough outer layers around the base and stem.

Using a mandolin, slice the artichokes paper-thin and transfer to medium bowl.

Squeeze the lemon halves over the artichokes, and toss with the oil. Sprinkle with salt, and use a potato peeler to shave the Parmesan over the salad. Serve in small bowls.

CANAPES
Serves 8

Genova is a little more formal, so canapes are served at the more refined establishments. Here's an easy recipe to use when you want to impress your guests.

2 (8-ounce) packages cream cheese
½ cup sundried tomatoes in oil
½ cup pesto (see recipe on page 107)
2 tablespoons Italian tuna in oil, (see Sources, page 234)
1½ tablespoons salt
12 pre-made 2-inch diameter tart shells, available online
12 2-inch diameter puff pastry shells, available online

Toppings:
¼ cup pancetta pieces
1 (2-ounce) can anchovies, drained (I like Roland brand— see Sources, page 234)
¼ cup parsley leaves
1 hardboiled quail egg, quartered
¼ cup chives
1 small tomato, quartered

Divide the cream cheese into 3 equal portions and place each portion in a separate small bowl. Puree or finely dice your sundried tomatoes.

Add 1 tablespoon pesto to one bowl of cream cheese, 1 tablespoon pureed sundried tomato into second bowl, and 2 tablespoons tuna to cream cheese in the third bowl. Add ½ teaspoon of salt to each mixture. Whisk all three mixtures in their separate bowls until smooth.

Place the mixtures into 3 separate piping bags, about 5 ounces per bag, and pipe the mixtures into alternating tart and pastry shells.

Cook the pancetta in a sauté pan for 3 to 5 minutes until crispy and drain on paper towels.

Top the tuna canapés with a 1-inch sliver of anchovy, the parsley, and quartered quail egg.

Top the sundried tomato canapés with the pancetta.

Top the pesto canapés with bits of tomato and chives and serve immediately.

DECONSTRUCTED CAPRESE SALAD

Serves 4

This lovely salad is a twist on a classic gazpacho. Because the tomato is pureed, it should be served with spoons.

1 cup day old bread, torn into pieces
¼ cup pesto (see recipe on next page)
1 cup (about 15) cherry tomatoes, halved
3 tablespoons olive oil
1 tablespoon lemon juice (about ½ a lemon)
½ teaspoon salt
1 cup fresh soft burrata cheese, quartered
Fresh basil, for garnish
¼ cup julienned sundried tomato, for garnish

In the bowl of a food processor, add the bread and pulse until breadcrumbs form.

In a small bowl, stir the breadcrumbs together with the pesto, and set aside.

In the cleaned bowl of the food processor, add the tomatoes, oil, lemon juice, and salt. Pulse 15 seconds, or until well combined, and set aside.

Working with 4 glasses (one per person), layer each glass first with the tomato puree, then the buratta, then the pesto breadcrumbs. Top each glass with a basil leaf and garnish with the sundried tomato strips. Serve immediately with spoons.

PESTO

Makes 1 cup

Pesto is very Ligurian. You will find it on everything from pasta to pizza, all over the region. I love it on fresh tomatoes with mozzarella, as an Apero nibble. In the summer, I always have a jar in the refrigerator. You'll notice the omission of garlic in this recipe—in Liguria and most of Northern Italy, garlic is not used in pesto.

4 cups fresh basil leaves
1 cup grated Parmesan cheese
1 cup olive oil
½ teaspoon salt

Place the basil, Parmesan cheese, oil, and salt into the bowl of a food processor fitted with a blade. Pulse for 3 minutes until it forms a paste. Set aside. You can make this ahead and refrigerate in a sealed container for up to 2 weeks.

PESTO, PREGO

Liguria, on the Italian Riviera, invented pesto. Pesto is the basil-based paste made from olive oil, pine nuts, and Parmesan cheese. Tons of chefs, including Mario Batali, have tried to import the Ligurian sweet basil back to America without any luck. I've been told that chefs have brought back seeds, plants—even Ligurian dirt—to see if they can grow the basil found only here on the coast. One interesting fact is the pesto in Liguria has no garlic added, like pestos made in most other regions. The truth is that on the Riviera very little garlic is used, period.

FRENCH 75

Serves 1

1 ounce gin
¼ ounce simple syrup (see page 46)
½ ounce lemon juice
2 ounces champagne

Combine the gin, syrup, and lemon juice in a cocktail shaker filled with ice. Shake vigorously and strain into a chilled champagne glass. Top with champagne, stir gently, and enjoy.

A WORD ABOUT WINE

It's perfectly fine to choose wine for your aperitivo; in fact, trying local varieties is encouraged. There are several varieties from this region. Of course Prosecco is popular, but varietal wines, such as Vermentino, Gavi, and Pigato are most popular, with crisp notes and hints of the sea. Try a glass of chilled local wine instead of a cocktail for an occasional aperitivo.

Many of the wines of this region are from grapes grown in the steeply-terraced vineyards along the Cinque Terra coastline. Italians also produce lovely rosé wines that are light and soft, and perfectly suited to hot summer evenings.

CAVO-MARESCOTTO SIGNATURE DRINK
Serves 1

This classic bar in the heart of Genova features an amazing signature drink. Truth be told, Italians are not that into signature drinks, but this cocktail was invented at this bar many years ago, and has become known for it. It's a smooth cocktail, with a beautiful amber color—very appetizing!

1 ½ ounces sweet vermouth
1 ounce vodka
½ ounce chartreuse

Fill a cocktail shaker with ice, add the vermouth, vodka, and chartreuse, and shake until chilled. Strain into a coupe, and serve.

GIN AND TONIC
Serves 1

This simple cocktail has made a huge comeback in the past five years. With many bars serving artisan gin, Italians have a method of the preparation and presentation of the two key ingredients. Hint: the serving glass is key.

Besides aperitivo, Italians have been known to serve this drink as an after-lunch beverage in the heat of the summer—it cools and refreshes the palate and lightens the stomach. Or so I am told.

2 ounces gin
3 ounces tonic water
1 lemon wedge

Place several ice cubes in a balloon glass and stir to chill the glass thoroughly, then add the gin and tonic and stir again. Garnish with a wedge of lemon.

SANTA MARGHERITA

Twenty-five years ago, we rented our first summer house in Santa Margherita. It was our introduction to the Italian Riviera. Our children were little and we spent six weeks in a hillside villa perched high above the town. It was our first time living on the Riviera for an extended period of time, and of course we were in love. We managed to enjoy the aperitivo hour every day after we returned from the beach, and those times are etched in our memories—so many good times in a beautiful setting.

Santa Margherita is located at the seaside, three kilometers from Portofino. It boasts all the bells and whistles of a Riviera lifestyle: glamour, fashion, and great food. This city, like Genova, boasts *trompe l'oeil* paintings on buildings. Shutters and moldings are sometimes painted on the buildings to look three-dimensional, when these details are not really there. This art form is the signature architectural element of this region of the Italian Riviera.

Just around the corner from Santa Margherita, roughly three miles away, is the jet-set haven of Portofino. It's a sliver of land compared to Santa Margherita, which is a full-blown mini-metropolis. Santa Margherita has markets, shopping, beautiful parks, broad pedestrian walking streets, and old-fashioned grand hotels. We enjoyed all the perks of Santa Margherita when we lived there. We lounged, napped, cooked, and spent most of our days at one of the beach clubs located on Paraggi Beach, situated between Portofino

and Santa Margherita. This popular tiny crescent of sandy beach was divided into three family-owned beach clubs.

One of the most useful perks of beach clubs are the tiny cabanas that visitors are provided. Cabanas are the only form of privacy for beach patrons. We would stuff all of our belongings in the tiny changing rooms, and change into our swimsuits in shifts, before heading to our rented beach chairs and umbrella.

We shared showers and ate lunch at the clubs alongside many Italians vacationing from Milano. It didn't matter that the guests were from different countries: we were just all families on safari, taking in the sights at the local watering hole. Much to our surprise and delight, an apero after a day at the beach could be enjoyed right on the beach at the beach club restaurant—so posh and so perfect.

Of course, Santa Margherita has many other options to sit and enjoy cocktails and nibbles. The beautiful Grand Hotel Miramare has an exquisite terrace that overlooks the sea. This Art Nouveau hotel reminds me of something Wes Anderson might use as movie set. Aperitivo there is classic and fancy. Its blue and white façade is a bright beacon on the seaside promenade.

Just past the Grand Hotel Miramare is an inlet with a variety of bars, all great places to grab an early evening nip. We often sat until the sunset, plotting where to grab some fried fish.

Santa Margherita has a lovely park that embraces the harbor like a giant hug. You can take a boat to nearby Portofino, and enjoy apero in two towns in one evening. Any way you choose to enjoy it, apero by the sea or at a beach club makes summer nights the best part of the day.

Opposite page, top: Bagni Rosa is a beach club across the street from the Hotel Miramare. Its elevated pink cabanas make it a distinctive landmark; below, some of the beaches are rocky, and popular for sunning and diving.

Above: Lovely pebble details are inlaid in the piazza and in front of churches throughout the city; All the beach clubs are along the main street. You can see the beaches from the main drag.

Detail of the monument to Christopher Columbus.

Floating bars are found on an inlet from the sea, where buildings painted in Trompe~l'œil line the waterside.

The Hotel Miramare's bright facade is very recognizable, it would make a great set for a Wes Anderson film.

ENDIVE FILLED WITH GORGONZOLA CHEESE
Serves 8

1 cup soft gorgonzola
16 endive leaves, washed and patted dry

Whisk the gorgonzola and place it into a piping bag.

Arrange the endive leaves on a serving plate, and pipe about
2 teaspoons cheese into the center of the leaf. Serve immediately.

CAMPARI SHAKERATO
Serves 1

*Shakerato refers to an Italian mixology technique when espresso, or a
cocktail, is placed into a shaker filled with fewer ice cubes than usual,
shaken, then strained into a chilled glass. It produces a finishing foam
to top off the glass. In this book, there are several cocktails that use this
method.*

1½ ounces Campari
5 ice cubes
½ ounce club soda
1 lemon peel

Fill a martini glass with ice, and set aside to chill.

Place the Campari into a cocktail shaker filled with 5 ice cubes,
and shake vigorously.

Dump the ice out of the martini glass, and strain the Campari into
the chilled glass, finish with a splash of club soda, add a twist of
lemon peel, and serve.

CYNAR NEGRONI

Serves 1

Italian Cynar is a bitter liqueur made from thirteen herbs and plants. Predominant among these is the artichoke (Cynara scolymus), from which the drink derives its name. Since 1995, Cynar has been manufactured and distributed by the Campari Group. Truth is that this liqueur has a softer taste and is less bitter than Campari, which is what is used in the traditional Negroni. Cynar is easy to order online to stock your Italian aperitivo bar (see Sources, page 234).

1 ounce Cynar
1 ounce sweet vermouth
1 ounce gin
1 twist lemon

Fill a highball glass with ice, add the Cynar, vermouth, and gin, and stir to combine. Garnish with a twist of lemon.

CUBE THEORY

For most cocktails in this book, and indeed for most cocktails using a shaker, you fill a shaker with ice cubes, not crushed ice. There is still room for the liquor, and the cubes don't melt as easily. Plus, it's way easier to strain into a glass. The Shakerato recipe is an exception to this rule, in that it calls for only 5 cubes of ice in the shaker. Don't worry, though, it will still be very cold when shaken!

PEACH BELLINI
Serves 2

Famous in Venice and throughout the Italian Riviera, this cocktail is a perfect use for seasonal summer peaches. I like to slice and freeze peaches when they are ripe so that I have them all summer for this cocktail. It is the perfect cocktail to serve with prosciutto and melon.

1 cup frozen fresh peaches
¼ cup peach Schnapps
1½ tablespoons powdered sugar
1 cup champagne, or prosecco

Place the frozen peaches, Schnapps, and sugar in a blender and mix until smooth. Divide the Bellini between 2 champagne flutes. Top each glass off with champagne or prosecco. Stir gently to combine, or not, as desired. Serve immediately.

FIG SLICES WITH SOFT CHEESE AND BALSAMIC VINEGAR DRIZZLE WITH MICRO GREENS
Serves 4

8 ripe figs
1 (8-ounce) wedge or wheel of ripe cheese, such as brie or Humboldt Fog or fresh Ricotta
3 tablespoons balsamic vinegar (I use Saba, which is a type of thicker, sweeter balsamic vinegar)
¼ cup micro greens
1 teaspoon flake salt (I use Maldon brand)

Slice the figs in half lengthwise, and arrange on a serving plate, cut side up. Place a small dollop of cheese on each half. Drizzle vinegar in a splatter pattern all over the figs, then sprinkle with micro greens, and the flake salt. Serve immediately.

SALAMI-FILLED PUFFS
Serves 12

These are the Italian version of that Southern party staple, pigs-in-a-blanket. Of course, I can never stop eating them; they really are the perfect aperitivo treat. Sometimes pasticceria (pastry shops) offer the best pastries of this type. Pasticceria Oneto is a great choice for these puffs, although any one of these pasticcerias on the pedestrian streets off piazza Caprera is a good choice.

1 sheet puff pastry
½ cup cream cheese (Fun fact: In Italy, cream cheese is called "Philadelphia.")
12 slices Genoa salami, cut in half

Preheat oven to 400°F.

Thaw the puff pastry and unroll it onto a board or surface covered with a sheet of parchment paper. Roll the pastry out to a 12 x 12-inch square. Spread the cream cheese to cover the top of the puff pastry.

With a sharp knife, cut the pastry into 3 x 3-inch squares. Place a half slice of salami on top of the pastry square (turn the square so it is a diamond shape with four points), and then fold the two side points of the diamond over the salami, just covering the salami in the middle. The salami half will stick out either end. Place on a baking sheet and bake 15 minutes until golden brown. Serve at room temperature.

SAVORY MASCARPONE ICE CREAM WITH BALSAMIC ROASTED GRAPES

Serves 4

This savory ice cream is the perfect counterpoint to the sweetness of the roasted grapes. You can add sweetness to the ice cream, if desired. Serve it as dessert with vin santo, or as an amaro after dinner.

Ice Cream:
1 ½ cups whole milk
1 ½ teaspoons unflavored powdered gelatin

1 cup mascarpone
Zest of 1 lemon, finely grated
½ teaspoon salt

Note: To make a sweet ice cream, add ¼ cup sugar when heating the milk and gelatin.

In a small saucepan, whisk the milk and gelatin together, and let stand for 5 minutes.

Warm the milk over medium heat, whisking until the gelatin dissolves. Remove the pan from the heat and whisk in the mascarpone and lemon zest until smooth.

Pour the ice cream base into a bowl and let it cool to room temperature. Pour the base into an ice cream maker and process according to the manufacturer's instructions. Scrape the ice cream into a container and freeze until set, at least 4 hours.

Balsamic Roasted Grapes:
2 cups red seedless grapes
2 tablespoons sugar
3 tablespoons good quality balsamic vinegar

Preheat oven to 400°F. On a cookie sheet, toss the grapes with sugar and balsamic, and roast for 20 minutes or until grapes are golden and soft. Set aside to cool to room temperature. May be made in advance and stored in an airtight container at room temperature for 24 hours.

To assemble, place a small scoop of ice cream in each of 4 small bowls, and top with roasted grapes. Serve immediately.

GRISSINI

Makes 32 (12-inch) long thin breadsticks

1 teaspoon active dry yeast
1 ¼ cups warm water, + ¼ cup to activate the yeast
½ tablespoon sugar
1 ¼ cups semolina flour
1 ½ cups Italian "Double Zero" flour, + 2 tablespoons to
  dust with
2 teaspoons salt
⅓ cup extra-virgin olive oil

Preheat the oven to 400°F.

Stir together the yeast, ¼ cup warm water, and the sugar in bowl
of mixer, and let stand 5 minutes, or until foamy. Add the semolina
flour to the yeast mixture, the "Double Zero" flour, salt, oil, and
the remaining 1 ¼ cups warm water, and mix at low speed until
a very soft dough forms. Increase the speed to medium and beat
5 minutes, scraping down the sides of bowl occasionally, until the
dough is soft, smooth, and elastic.

Scrape the dough into the center of bowl and dust with 2 addi-
tional tablespoons "Double Zero" flour. Cover the bowl with
plastic wrap and let the dough rise for 1 ½ hours, or until it has
doubled.

Line 2 large baking sheets with parchment paper.

When the dough has doubled, punch it down and turn it out onto
a floured surface. Divide the dough into 2 equal portions. Cover
1 portion with plastic wrap, and cut the other portion into 16
equal pieces. Roll each of these pieces into a 15- to 16-inch-long
rope, about ⅛-inch thick. Place the ropes ½ inch apart on a baking
sheet, then repeat the process with the remaining dough and
arrange those ropes on the other baking sheet.

Bake 30 to 35 minutes, or until the grissini are pale golden and
crisp. Transfer to racks to cool. Grissini will keep for 3 days in a
sealed container.

PORTOFINO

Portofino is a popular aperitivo destination, and your chance to feel like a jetsetter, and rub elbows with the rich and famous. You will be part of the yacht crowd as you settle in at a floating bar and sip an Americana Shakerato.

Every trip to the Riviera must include the ultimate luxury destination—Portofino. We rented a house in the next town over, Santa Margherita, for years, and it became our apero ritual to go to Portofino at least once a week. We would take a 15-minute boat ride into the tiny marina of Portofino and grab a cocktail or two at a couple of bars on the bay.

Founded by the Romans and named *Portus Delphini*, or Port of the Dolphin, because of the large number of dolphins that inhabited the Tigullian Gulf until around the tenth century, Portofino became a resort destination for the elite in the 1950s. Yachts would dock at the tiny port so that the moneyed and celebrity guests could enjoy the handful of exclusive bars and restaurants. To this day the Portofino Yacht Club holds court to many movie stars and celebrities.

People-watching in Portofino is a main event around the port, and La Gritta American Bar is the perfect aperitivo destination. It's located across from the Yacht Club and is one of Italy's most famous jetset hangouts. La Gritta has played host to Frank Sinatra, John Wayne, Jackie O, Kate Blanchet, Hugh Jackman, Rod Stewart, P Diddy, and Beyonce, to name but a few from their autographed photos hung on the walls. Order a Negroni—it's simply chic. One of my favorite activities is to wander to the Yacht Club and watch the mega yachts dock in the tiny port. The gymnastic maneuvers needed to dock a mega yacht into a tight slip is a wonder to watch.

There's not much to Portofino as far as size, but something about its charms and reputation makes having a cocktail and a nibble overlooking the yacht club and marina very appealing. Maybe it's the fact that so many chic people populate such a small patch of land.

The Splendido Hotel in the main square is a great place to grab a cocktail when the sun goes down. You will most likely see some celebrities partaking in a cocktail or two here, as well.

If you want to see some sights before apero, you can hike to Castello Brown at the top of the cliff overlooking the harbor. It's a house museum of architectural interest that's open to the public and the view is great to see just before sunset.

Portofino is only three kilometers from Santa Margherita, but the winding road that connects these two Riviera towns is a treacherous narrow passage that makes the drive very exciting. It's fun on the way over, but drive carefully on your way back from apero.

Whether you're enjoying aperitivo at a bayside bar—or seaside on your yacht or boat deck as many people do—sipping an Aperol spritz is the great equalizer, and popular with everyone.

La Gritta American Bar is the best place to park yourself for the ultimate people-watching and celebrity-spotting experience. It boasts vintage décor and walls filled with celebrity photos. Above: the barman at Bar Gritta.

CAMPARI WITH BLOOD ORANGE ICE CUBES
Serves 1

I love this idea! I not only freeze blood orange juice ice cubes, but I make juice popsicles all summer long, and I pour a little Campari into a glass, dip my popsicle into it, and once it starts to melt, the drink is perfection. I also refrigerate my Campari, which keeps it at a perfect temperature to enjoy on a hot summer day.

2 cups blood orange juice
1½ ounces Campari

Pour the blood orange juice into an ice tray, or into popsicle forms, and freezer for at least 4 hours.

Pour the Campari into a highball glass, add 3 blood orange ice cubes (or popsicle), and enjoy.

KIR ROYALE
Serves 1

⅓ ounce Crème de Cassis
3 ounces good chilled champagne

In a champagne flute, add the Crème di Cassis, fill the glass with champagne, and serve.

FRESH MOZZARELLA WITH BASIL ON A BED OF TOMATO COULIS

Serves **8**

Tomato Coulis
Yields 2 cups

4 tomatoes
1 teaspoon salt

2 cups tomato coulis (recipe below)
4 cups fresh mozzarella
1 cup fresh basil chiffonade

Remove the stem end, and score an X into the tomato skin with a sharp knife.

Fill a medium pot with water and heat to boiling over medium-high heat. Drop the whole tomatoes into the boiling water, and cook 30 seconds to 1 minute, until the skins start to come loose around the score marks.

Transfer the tomatoes to a bowl of ice water to shock them, then peel and dice them.

Place a large mesh strainer over a bowl, add the diced tomatoes, and sprinkle with salt. After about 30 minutes, puree the strained tomatoes with a hand blender (I like to keep the tomato water and reserve it for Bloody Marys). Refrigerate in sealed container until ready to use.

To assemble, use 8 small rimmed plates, and place 2 tablespoons of coulis on each plate, then top with ½ cup fresh mozzarella, and garnish each plate with ½ teaspoon basil.

OPEN-FACE PROSCIUTTO FINGER SANDWICH WITH HOMEMADE AIOLI

Serves 4

Homemade Aioli:

Makes ½ cup

I clove garlic
I large egg yolk, room
   temperature
2 teaspoons fresh lemon
   juice

½ teaspoon Dijon mustard
¼ cup extra-virgin olive oil
3 tablespoons vegetable oil
Salt and pepper to taste

Focaccia (recipe on page 74)
2 cups baby arugula
¼ pound prosciutto, thinly
   sliced

4 hardboiled eggs, sliced
I teaspoon salt

To make the Aioli, use the flat blade of a large heavy knife to mash the garlic clove to a paste, transfer to a small bowl, add a pinch of salt, and set aside.

In a medium bowl, whisk together the yolk, lemon juice, and mustard.

In another bowl, combine the oils, and add a few drops at a time into the yolk mixture, whisking constantly until all the oil is incorporated, and the mixture has emulsified. (If the mixture separates, stop adding the oil and continue whisking until it comes together, then continue to add any remaining oil.)

Whisk in the garlic paste and season with salt and pepper. If the aioli is too thick, whisk in I or 2 drops of water to thin it. Cover and refrigerate until ready to use. Aioli can be made up to I week in advance and kept in a sealed container in the refrigerator.

To assemble, spread the aioli over the top of the focaccia bread, top with the arugula, prosciutto, the sliced eggs, and sprinkle with salt. Cut the focaccia into 8 (2 to 3-inch) squares, and serve immediately.

TUNA CREAM SPOONS WITH EDIBLE FLOWERS

Serves 6

Italians love canned tuna—it's apparent when you're in the grocery store, where you find a complete aisle of canned tuna of all types. It's almost certain you will find a version of tuna salad or tuna crème on any aperitivo menu anywhere in Italy. This version uses edible flowers as garnish, which is an appetizing way to garnish these nibbles. Note: These can't be made ahead because the pastry spoons will absorb the moisture and become sticky.

½ **cup heavy cream**
1 **(5 ounce) can Italian tuna in oil**
¼ **cup prepared mayonnaise**
½ **teaspoon sea salt**
1 **teaspoon finely chopped shallots**
18 **(3 per person) edible spoons (see Sources, page 234)**
1 **cup edible flowers, such as rosemary, chive flowers, or pansies**

In the bowl of processor, combine the heavy cream, tuna, mayonnaise, salt, and chopped shallots. Pulse until the mixture is the consistency of whipped cream.

Transfer to a piping bag, and pipe the tuna cream into the edible spoons. Top each spoon with an edible flower and arrange on a serving dish. Serve immediately.

BLACK RISOTTO CAKES
WITH SALSA AND CRÈME FRAÎCHE

Serves 8 to 10

6 cups vegetable stock
⅓ cup extra-virgin olive oil, divided
¼ cup unsalted butter, divided
2 shallots, minced
2 cups black rice
1½ cups white wine
½ cup Parmesan
Salt and freshly ground black pepper to taste
1 cup crème fraîche

Salsa:
2 large Roma tomatoes, chopped and drained in a strainer
¼ cup finely chopped onion
½ cup finely chopped basil
¼ cup olive oil
½ teaspoon salt
3 tablespoons balsamic vinegar

Toss all salsa ingredients together and set aside until ready to use.

To make the risotto, warm the broth in a medium pot over low heat. Keep at a bare simmer while you do the next step.

In a large heavy pan with high sides, heat 2 tablespoons olive oil and 2 tablespoons butter over medium heat. Add the shallots and cook 3 to 5 minutes, until translucent. Add the rice, toss to coat with the butter and oil, and cook for 3 minutes.

Using a ladle, alternate between the broth and wine, adding one ladle at a time of each, and stirring until each ladle is incorporated into the rice before adding more liquid. Cook 25 to 30 minutes, until all the broth is absorbed. Add salt and pepper to taste.

Fold in the Parmesan cheese, then turn out onto a baking sheet and refrigerate for 1 hour. When chilled, use a 2-inch diameter round cookie cutter to cut the risotto into round cakes.

Gather the scraps and flatten into rounds, using the cookie cutter to incorporate all the rice possible.

Heat the remaining olive oil in a large sauté pan over medium-high heat. Place the risotto rounds into the hot pan and cook 2 to 3 minutes per side, until brown. Drain on paper towels and serve warm with a dollop of crème fraîche and salsa.

AMERICANO SHAKERATO
Serves 1

1½ ounces sweet vermouth
1½ ounces Campari
1 orange peel

Chill a martini glass with ice, then discard the ice.

Place the vermouth and Campari into a cocktail shaker filled with ice, shake, and strain into the chilled martini glass. Garnish with an orange peel.

POLENTA CAKES WITH CAVIAR
Serves 6

4 cups water
1 cup polenta (not the instant kind), usually found at local Latin markets
1 teaspoon salt
¼ cup olive oil, for grilling
1 (2.2 ounce) jar caviar, or fish roe
1 cup crème fraîche

In a large pot over medium-high heat, bring 4 cups water to a brisk boil. Pour the polenta into the boiling water, and add the salt, whisking constantly for 30 to 40 minutes, until the polenta thickens.

Use a spatula to spread the polenta out about ½-inch thick onto a 13 x 9-inch rimmed sheet pan, and refrigerate for 1 hour, or until cool.

Heat a grill to medium-high.

Once the polenta is cool and firm, cut into 2-inch squares. Brush the squares with oil, and grill 3 minutes on each side.

Place the grilled polenta squares on a platter and top with dollops of caviar and crème fraîche.

Serve at room temperature.

LEVANTO

This mostly overlooked hip town is also on the path to Cinque Terra. Levanto is a great place to spend a day or a weekend. The aperitivo culture is super casual, and you'll find the best bars on the beach where the views are spectacular. Sip and watch the sea kayaks glide by.

Levanto is the sleepy little seaside Riviera town on the out-skirts of the famed Cinque Terre. It is home to summer vaca-tioners, surfers, and active young families. Making your way down winding roads into town, you'll pass a luminous carpet of olive groves.

When you reach town "centro" (center), you'll pass the train station that takes you to the famous Cinque Terra, and then you are funneled onto a beautiful, bustling, tree-lined main street that dead-ends at the beachfront.

The seaside boardwalk has large luscious gardens, with tow-ering pine trees at one end and an expansive sandy beach at the other. A distinctive collection of small rowboats covered with blue and white striped tarps sit on the beachfront in a pleasing painterly pattern, and have become the unique visual trademark of Levanto.

After dinner, you can enjoy a *passeggiata* (a walk) along the curved boardwalk, and take in the many stately villas and the dreamy gardens.

This town holds a special place for me and for my family. Levanto was one of the first places our family rented a house to summer on the Italian Riviera. It has a great family vibe and became the perfect summer place for us for many years. We soon grew to love the town and its laid-back attitude . . . as well as its seaside aperitivi.

The sparkling waters attract snorkelers from all around the world. When the weather turns stormy and the sea is rough, surfers take over the town to ride the big waves.

Most Riviera towns have many family-owned and operated beach clubs, but Levanto has a large sandy beach with just one large beach club. It looks very different than other beachfront towns.

The four elevated beach shacks are a great place to enjoy apero in the late afternoon, a great time to sip a cocktail and watch the kayaks paddle along the shoreline. One of my favorite places is The Casino Beach club, with two Olympic-size pools, and a patch of sand with a great bar at ground level. Grab a seat and watch the action poolside with an Aperol Spritz Shakerato in hand.

Unlike other Riviera towns, Levanto's lazy lifestyle reminds me of the energy of a California beach town. The difference of course is its distinctive and traditional Italian look. Levanto has a good share of tourists, but you never feel like it's filled to the brim with vacationers. It's my personal secret Riviera destination, and not to be missed on your Italian Riviera aperitivo tour.

Previous page: The bay at Levanto is surrounded with breathtaking private villas and gardens. The villa pictured overlooks one of many public beaches that dot the bay.

Opposite page: You know you're in Levanto if the boats are covered in trademark blue and white canvas covers.

SPINACH PIE

Serves 6 to 8

Vegetable pies, or tortas, are traditional throughout the region of Liguria, and they usually make an appearance at apero time. This recipe is used for the classic Easter torta of Liguria.

Crust:
4 cups all-purpose flour
I cup olive oil
I tablespoon salt
¾ cups very cold water

To prepare the crust, place the flour in the bowl of a food processor, and add the oil and salt. Pulse until the dough becomes pebble-sized crumbs, and continue to pulse, adding a little water at a time, until the dough comes together to form a soft ball. If needed, add more water to reach the desired consistency. Set the dough aside and make the filling.

Filling:
3 tablespoons olive oil
½ medium red onion, thinly sliced
6 cups chopped fresh spinach
½ teaspoon salt
½ teaspoon white pepper
I cup grated Parmesan
3 cups fresh ricotta cheese
I tablespoon dried marjoram
I egg

Preheat the oven to 375°F.

In a large sauté pan over medium heat, heat the olive oil and sauté the red onion slices for 3 to 5 minutes, or until the onions are transparent. Stir in the spinach, salt, and pepper and continue to cook 10 minutes, or until the spinach is wilted. Quickly cook off as much liquid left in the pan as possible, then remove the pan from the heat and set aside to cool slightly.

(continued on page 156)

In a large bowl, stir together the cheeses, marjoram, and the egg.

When the spinach mixture has cooled for about 10 minutes, squeeze any excess liquid from the mixture. Transfer the spinach to the cheese mixture, stir until well combined, and set aside.

Divide the dough into two equal parts, and flour a board or work surface. Roll one portion of the dough out to a rectangle to fit the bottom and sides of a 6 x 10-inch baking pan, making sure the dough is about ¼-inch thick. Make sure the edges of the dough extend up the sides of the dish. Fill with the spinach mixture, and smooth the top with a spoon.

Roll out the remaining dough and place on top of the spinach. Pinch all around the edges to seal the crust. Bake for 1 hour, or until the crust begins to brown.

To serve, cut into 2-inch squares and serve at room temperature.

FOCACCIA CANAPES, WITH OLIVE TAPENADE
Serves 10 to 12

Focaccia (page 74)

Olive Tapenade
Makes 2 cups

2 cups pitted green olives
1 clove garlic
2 tablespoons capers
¼ cup fresh basil leaves
3 tablespoons extra-virgin olive oil

To make the Tapenade, place all the ingredients in a food processor and pulse just until coarsely combined. Tapenade may be made ahead and refrigerated in an airtight container for up to two weeks.

Spread the focaccia bread with the tapenade, cut into 1-inch squares, arrange on a platter, and serve at room temperature.

MUSHROOM SALAD

Serves 6

Since there is a good bit of vinegar in the recipe, this is a bit of a pickled salad. It is served at room temperature, but I like it cold as well.

4 tablespoons olive oil
5 cups small Portabello mushrooms, trimmed and cut into ½-inch slices
¼ cup minced onion
1 clove garlic, minced
¼ cup red wine vinegar
½ teaspoon salt
½ cup chopped parsley leaves, for garnish

In a large skillet over medium heat, add 3 tablespoons oil and the mushrooms, and cook 5 to 7 minutes, stirring occasionally, until the mushrooms release the liquid and begin to brown. Decrease the heat to low, add the onion and garlic, and sauté 3 minutes, or until the onion is translucent.

Transfer the mushrooms to a bowl, stir in the vinegar, the remaining tablespoon oil, and the salt. Serve at room temperature, garnished with parsley.

This recipe can be made a day in advance and refrigerated in a sealed container until ready to serve.

LEMON HUMMUS

Serves 8+

I love to serve this with vegetable sticks, such as carrots or radishes; and of course it is perfect with Grissini (page 130).

**2 cups well-cooked or canned chickpeas, drained and
    liquid reserved**
½ cup tahini (sesame paste), plus some of its oil
¼ cup extra-virgin olive oil, plus more for drizzling
2 cloves garlic, peeled
1 teaspoon salt
Juice of 1 lemon
1 teaspoon lemon zest
Pinch of cumin or paprika
Chopped fresh parsley leaves, for garnish

Put all the ingredients except the parsley into the bowl of a food processor and pulse. While pulsing, add the chickpea liquid as needed to achieve a smooth puree. Taste and adjust the seasoning.

Drizzle with the olive oil and sprinkle with cumin or paprika, and top with the parsley. Serve with your choice of vegetables or breadsticks for dipping.

ITALIAN GARDEN SANDWICH
Serves 8

I love to serve this sandwich in the late afternoon with glass of chilled white wine. It's also a wonderful picnic food, if you want to plan an aperitivo on-the-go.

1 large boule (a round loaf of bread)
3 tablespoons pesto (page 107)
6 roasted red peppers (store-bought works fine)
½ red onion, peeled and thinly sliced
12 fresh basil leaves
2 large balls fresh Mozzarella, thinly sliced
1 cup sundried tomatoes in oil, drained and julienned
3 fresh tomatoes, thinly sliced
2 cups arugula
¼ pound prosciutto
¼ pound salami
½ teaspoon salt
½ teaspoon pepper

Cut the bread horizontally through the middle. Scoop out the inside of the loaf, top and bottom, leaving just the shell. (Save the bread to toast for bread crumbs later.) Brush the inside of the shells top and bottom with the pesto.

Layer half of all the ingredients into the bottom half, using the red peppers, the onions, and so on until the bread bowl is filled to the top. Next, fill the top half of the loaf, using the remaining fillings and layering them one at a time.

Cover the bottom half with the top, and tightly wrap with plastic wrap. Place in the refrigerator and use heavy weights to press the loaf—I use nested cast iron skillets for weights.) Refrigerate overnight, or for at least 5 hours before serving.

When you serve, remove the wrap, and use a serrated knife to cut the loaf into 1-inch slices, and arrange the slices on a platter with the layers showing.

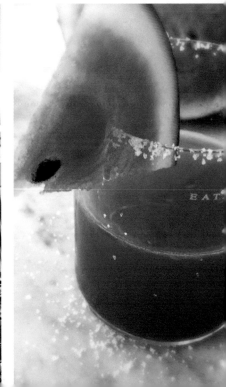

DIECI E LODE

Serves 1

1 ounce Campari	**1 ounce grapefruit juice**
2 ounces gin	**1 lime wedge**

Fill a cocktail shaker with ice and add the Campari, gin, and grapefruit juice. Shake vigorously and strain into a coupe. Garnish with a wedge of lime before serving.

WATERMELON MARGARITA

Serves 6

In Italy, seasonal cocktails are offered all along the seaside. This is a favorite when watermelon is in season. American cocktails, such as Margaritas, are very fashionable and available on most every menu.

1 cup sugar	**2 cups white or silver**
1 cup water	**tequila**
3 wide strips orange peel	**Salt, for rimming the glasses**
8 cups watermelon cubes	**6 small watermelon wedges,**
1 cup fresh lime juice	**for garnish**

In a small saucepan over high heat, bring the sugar, water, and orange peel to a boil. Reduce the heat to low and simmer 3 minutes, until the sugar dissolves. Transfer the syrup to a bowl to cool and discard the orange peel.

In a blender, puree the watermelon cubes until smooth. Strain through a fine-mesh strainer placed over a serving pitcher, pressing on the solids (you should have about 1 cup juice). Stir in the syrup, lime juice, and tequila.

Rim 6 glasses with salt, fill them with ice, then pour in the margarita mixture. Garnish with watermelon wedges.

Levanto has one the largest beach clubs on the Riviera and their bar boasts a huge cocktail menu, including a watermelon Margarita. An enormous public park across from the beach club offers family activities, including blowing giant bubbles. The park also has the best Gelateria in town.

PASTIS AND WATER

Serves 1

Pastis is the national aperitif of France—it is a combination of star anise, both black and white pepper corns, cardamom, sage, nutmeg, cloves, cinnamon, licorice, and a little sugar. When mixed with water it turns a milky white color. Italians on the Riviera have adopted this cocktail. The French Riviera is right up the road so it's not surprising that this popular French classic is enjoyed by their neighbors.

2 ounces Pastis
1 cup cold water

Pour the Pastis into a tall tumbler, and serve with a small pitcher of chilled water on the side. Pour water over the Pastis to individual taste.

APEROL SPRITZ SHAKERATO

Serves 1

Shakerato simply means "shaken." Shaken vigorously. The agitation of drinks forms a desired foam, and this technique is used in many classic drinks to add a little foam. Almost anything can be a shakerato— Campari, Vermouth, or, as in this recipe, the refreshing Italian spirit called Aperol.

3 ounces Aperol
2 ounces prosecco
1 ounce club soda

Fill a cocktail shaker with ice cubes, Aperol, prosecco, and soda.

Close and shake vigorously. Strain into a tall wine glass, and top with the foam.

LERICI

This little hamlet very near the Cinque Terra is mostly overlooked by the hordes of tourists. For many famous English writers of the 1800s and early 1900s—such as Mary and Percy Shelley, Lord Byron, and Keats—this was the place to be seen. It boasts one of the prettiest bays, the perfect setting for a late afternoon cocktail.

Lerici is a lovely seaside hamlet with a distinctive crescent-shaped piazza facing the sea. It has a curvilinear boardwalk. It was the favorite vacation spot of British writers for centuries; however, the unfortunate drowning here of Percy Shelly gave Lerici its nickname, the Golfo dei Poeti, meaning the Poets' Bay. It is also known as the Golfo of la Spezia.

From Lerici, it's a quick trip by boat to the Cinque Terre or Portovenere, and the boats run all day long into early evening. You can be back in time for aperitivo along Lerici's quiet bay. The boardwalk has a variety of bars, both classic and contemporary, to enjoy people-watching and local cocktail menus.

The bay is an active playground for yachts and sailing boats, and is dotted with fishing boats and narrow piers. The coastline is rugged and lined with jagged cliffs, a dramatic landscape that takes your breath away as you drive up the coast.

One must-see destination for cocktails is the exclusive beach club Eco del Mare. This hippy-chic boutique hotel makes you feel like a pampered castaway. The bar and reception are at the bottom of an amazing congregation of cliffs, with a steep drop to the beach below. The easy way down to this Riviera paradise is aboard a dark and groovy elevator that leaves from a parking lot above the beach.

With only a tiny sliver of beach tucked into the rock forma-
tions, you'll feel like Sophia Loren or Marcello Mastroianni reliving
the Riviera lifestyle of 1962. Ask the barman to fix you the trop-
ical cocktail of the day, while you settle into a calm state, with
the sea lapping at your toes. When the sun goes down the locals
come out and you can people-watch to your heart's content while
nibbling and sipping a drink.

This small, down~to~earth seaside town is a
find. There are several bars on the narrow
pier where you can enjoy a cocktail with the
locals and raise a glass to the memory of
Shelly, who loved it here.

TUNA SALAD TEA SANDWICHES
Serves 8

Little sandwiches are a typical aperitivo snack on the Riviera. I know it sounds a little like an old-fashioned ladies luncheon, but these are definitely not that. Use good tuna and homemade aioli and these little bites become the perfect savory compliment to any cocktail. I sometimes wonder if the tea sandwiches are a throwback to the large English community that resided along the Riviera at the turn of the twentieth century—I'll bet they are!

1 (7 ounce) can fine quality Italian tuna in oil (I like Rio Mare brand)
2 tablespoons finely chopped red onion
2 tablespoons capers
1 teaspoon lemon juice
½ teaspoon sea salt
Chopped chives, optional
¼ cup homemade Aioli (page 143)
8 slices white bread

Use a fork to mix all the ingredients—except bread slices, of course—together in a bowl.

Lay out 4 slices of bread and spread 3 tablespoons of tuna on each piece, Cover with another piece of white bread. Cut the crusts off, and divide each sandwich into 4 triangles. Serve on a platter, garnished with chopped chives if you choose.

Opposite: The magnificent Lerici Castle rises on a rocky promontory overlooking the Bay of Lerici.

GRILLED SCALLOPS WITH PANCETTA

Serves 4

Scallops are abundant at the seaside. I am a fan of wrapping them in pancetta—salty pancetta and sweet scallops are a perfect flavor combination. I enjoy them with a glass of crisp rosé.

8 twigs rosemary, for skewers
8 fresh scallops
4 slices pancetta, cut in half
3 tablespoons olive oil

To make the rosemary skewers, remove the needles from the lower half of each twig of rosemary, and cut the bottom of the twig at a diagonal to form a sharp end.

Wrap each scallop with ½ strip of pancetta, leaving the top and bottom open, so that you can sear the scallop.

In a frying pan or skillet, warm the oil over medium-high heat and place the scallops on their side to crisp. Use tongs to turn the scallops so they evenly cook. Sear the scallops 1½ minutes on each side, until golden brown.

Arrange the scallops on a small plate and skewer each with a sprig of rosemary. Serve warm.

VERMOUTH SPRITZER

Serves 1

1 ounce dry vermouth
1½ ounces Cocchi Americano
3 ounces club soda
1 orange slice

Fill a highball glass with ice, and add the vermouth and Cocchi Americano. Stir to chill, top off with the club soda, and garnish with an orange slice.

FRIED BACALA
WITH POTATO PUREE AND PESTO
Serves 4

Bacala, or salted cod, is a bit of a poor man's fish and generally not a favorite dish in Italy. However, I tasted this while enjoying a Bicicletta cocktail and the lovely flavor of the pesto gives the fried fish just the right kick. You will probably find this fish in an Italian specialty store, or your farmers' market, or you can substitute fresh talapia.

Pesto:
1 cup fresh basil leaves
¼ cup grated **Parmesan**
½ teaspoon salt
½ cup olive oil

Potato Puree:
3 potatoes, peeled, and cut into large chunks
¼ cup heavy cream
2 teaspoons melted butter
½ teaspoon salt

For the Pesto: Combine all ingredients in the bowl of a food processor and pulse until just combined. Be careful not to over-process, as this will cause it to turn brown.

For the Potato Puree: Place the potatoes in a medium pot with enough water to cover and bring to a boil over medium-high heat.

Cook 15 to 20 minutes, or until the potatoes are soft when poked with a fork. If the water begins to boil over, lower the heat to medium.

In a small pot over low heat, warm the cream, butter, and salt, and stir to combine.

Drain the potatoes, and use a potato masher to mash by hand. Add the warm cream and butter and mash until the puree is smooth.

Bacala:
1 pound dried **Bacala (salted cod)**
1 cup flour
2 cups olive oil, or vegetable oil
1 teaspoon salt, for sprinkling

(continued on page 176)

The best method for soaking Bacala is to place the fish in a large bowl and cover with approximately 2 inches cold water. Cover, and put the bowl in the refrigerator for to 2 to 3 days, changing the water at least once a day to allow the fish to rehydrate.

When you are ready to cook, pat the cod dry with paper towels. Cut into 2- to 3-inch pieces and dredge each piece in the flour.

Heat the oil in a large skillet over high heat, and fry in batches, 3 to 5 minutes per side, or until both sides are golden brown. Remove carefully with a spatula and drain the fish on paper towels.

To assemble, use 4 small serving dishes, and place a dollop of potato puree on each. Drizzle with the pesto, and top with a couple of pieces of the fried Bacala. Sprinkle with salt.

Note: it seems like salted cod should already be salty, but the soaking leaches out most, so you can be liberal with adding extra.

LIMONCELLO MARGARITA
Serves 1

I actually invented this cocktail for friends while I was in Italy. I was asked to cook something very American. It was May 5th, so of course I opted for chili, guacamole, and chips with quesadillas. The sweet tartness of the limoncello is perfect with spicy food. Caution: This is a very strong cocktail—more than one and you're on your own. You've been warned.

1½ ounces tequila
1 ounce limoncello
1 ounce lemon juice
½ ounce triple sec, or orange-flavored liquor
1 lemon slice

Fill a glass with ice, then add the tequila, limoncello, lemon juice, and triple sec. Stir to chill and serve with a lemon garnish.

BICICLETTA
Serves 1

This is a go-to cocktail for me. When I have a little leftover white wine, it's an easy and delicious cocktail to whip up.

2 ounces Campari
2 ounces dry white wine
1 ounce club soda
1 orange slice

Add Campari and white wine to a wine glass. Add ice and top with soda. Stir gently and garnish with an orange slice.

HOTEL ECO DEL MARE

Eco Del Mare Hotel in Lerici is on one of the most picturesque beaches I have ever visited. It's got a natural bohemian feel. The hotel is situated in an incredibly rugged cove. The sea is blue and the bar is carved into a cave that resembles a natural grotto, and furnished with natural hammocks and driftwood picnic tables. It is truly unique—I could hang out there forever. Its full service bar and restaurant is sublime, featuring local fish and Ligurian specialties. Once you ride down the elevator to sea level, you will be enchanted. It's simply the best apero spot on the southern coast of the Italian Rivera. Make a point to visit and stay awhile.

ECO PASSION COCKTAIL
Serves 1

This was one of my favorite "cocktails of the day" at the hotel bar. The barman prepared it with such finesse I could not take my eyes off him. When he cut the ripe passion fruit in half, sprinkled it with raw sugar, and pulled out a blow torch to caramelize the sugar-dipped passion fruit, I was enraptured. Poured over crushed ice, this is all things I love about specialty cocktails: it's cold, perfumed, well-balanced, and that caramelized passion fruit garnish is truly a genius touch. If you don't have a blowtorch, use a lighter to caramelize the passion fruit.

2 ounces vodka
Pulp of 2 passion fruit
1 teaspoon sugar
2 ounces sparkling water

½ ounce pineapple juice
½ passion fruit, halved
½ teaspoon sugar
crushed ice

Fill a cocktail shaker with ice, and add the vodka, pulp, sugar, sparkling water, and pineapple juice. Shake furiously. Strain into a highball glass filled with crushed ice.

Sprinkle the passion fruit with the sugar, and flame with a blow torch or lighter just until the sugar caramelizes. Garnish the cocktail with the passion fruit.

SHRIMP AND ARTICHOKES WITH WALNUT VINAIGRETTE

from Hotel Eco Del Mare
Serves 4

1 quart water
3 artichokes, cleaned and cut into quarters
12 shrimp, peeled and deveined
½ cup chopped walnuts
¼ cup walnut oil
¼ cup balsamic vinegar
½ teaspoon salt
½ teaspoon pepper
3 tablespoons fresh thyme
1 lemon, cut into 4 wedges

Bring the water to a boil in a large pot over medium-high heat. When the water is boiling, drop in the artichokes, and blanch for 8 minutes, then remove with a slotted spoon and set aside on paper towels.

In the same pot of boiling water, add the shrimp, and cook 1 minute, or just until pink. Remove with a slotted spoon and transfer to a colander to drain.

Heat the oven to 350°F.

Toast the walnuts in a shallow pan about 5 minutes, watching carefully so they don't burn.

In a large bowl, whisk together the walnut oil and vinegar and toss with the artichokes, shrimp, toasted walnuts, salt, and pepper. Set aside to cool to room temperature before serving. Divide among 4 small plates, and garnish each plate with fresh thyme and a squeeze of lemon.

FRIED CHICKPEA CAKES

from Hotel Eco Del Mare
Serves 8

2 tablespoons olive oil
½ white onion, diced
1 quart water, or chicken or vegetable stock
2¼ cups chickpea flour
1 teaspoon salt
3 to 4 cups vegetable oil, for frying and oiling the cake pan
1 teaspoon flake salt (I use Maldon)

Oil an 11 x 9-inch cake pan and set aside.

In a sauté pan over medium heat, add the olive oil and sauté the onions 3 to 5 minutes, until translucent.

While the onions cook, bring the water (or stock) to a boil in medium pot over medium-high heat. When it reaches a boil, whisk in the chickpea flour, salt, and the onion. Cook 10 to 12 minutes, until the mixture thickens.

Spread the chickpea mixture into the oiled cake pan and refrigerate 1 hour, or until set. You can also prepare this 1 day in advance and keep refrigerated until ready to serve.

When you are ready to serve, cut the chickpea into 1½-inch squares.

Heat the vegetable oil in a cast iron skillet, and fry the squares 3 to 5 minutes on each side, until crispy. Transfer to paper towels to drain, sprinkle with flake salt, and serve warm.

PORTOVENERE

This tiny seaside town is just a few miles down the coast from Cinque Terra, and not to be missed. The gentle curve of the seaside boardwalk and the sweeping views of the castle above will have you lingering by the sea and sipping cocktails until dinnertime.

This stunning Italian Riviera destination is tiny but leaves a big impression. As you wind down the hairpin roads from La Spezia, you're headed to the farthest peninsula on the Italian Rivera. The village is at the most southern end of a peninsula breaking away from the jagged coastline of the Riviera di Levante, that forms the western tip of the Gulf of La Spezia. The drive to Portovenere is precarious, but it's worth the effort. As you enter the town, the view of the port is altogether stunning, colorful, and lively.

Portovenere seems literally enveloped by a mountain and has only two main streets. One road leads to the Doria Castle and the gothic church of Saint Peter, and the other runs along the sea. You will want to climb the narrow cliff-lined walkways from the sea to Doria Castle; the glorious views and ancient porticos of the castle are worth experiencing. I love taking guests up to the castle and seeing their faces as they look through the porticos to see the waves crashing against the jagged shoreline below—it's so dramatic and cinematic.

The boardwalks situated along the bay are among the most active on the Riviera. Sunbathing and swimming in the gulf along the rocks is a must, and rowing and sailing are both popular water sports in the summer. Sailing regattas are held several times a year. As the sun sets behind the massive mountain backdrop to this quaint village, every bar is packed to the brim with locals enjoying aperitivo.

At the end of the peninsula are three small islands: Palmaria, Tino, and Tinetto; and only Palmaria Island, which lies directly opposite the village of Portovenere beyond a narrow strait, is partially inhabited. Be sure to take a water taxi to Palmaria to enjoy an aperitivo and dinner at the famed Locanda Lorena—the taxi ride also provides exciting views of both Portovene and Palmaria.

One of my favorite Portovenere bars, La Vigna Di Nettuno has a modern feel, with cocktails endlessly flowing and techno music pumping. Be forewarned that sometimes it's so busy one must wait a bit for a drink, which is okay because the music and cocktails are worth it.

Portovenere by night, seen from a boat on the way to Locanda Lorena. Boats are available for rent, and this is the best place to take a ferry to Cinque Terra. The ticket stand is on the boardwalk—you can't miss it.

CHARCUTERIE PLATE PRIMER

1. The Board
Pick out a wooden board—the bigger, the better. Of course, gauge your crowd—24 x 30 inches is perfect for a gathering of eight people.

I find beautiful cheese and cutting boards at flea markets. You can also use cake stands for a different look. Make sure you have plenty of spreaders, spoons, and forks all over the board for ease of serving. I also like to put bowls and plates on top of the board for some height and textural interest. I put the bowls on the board first as a great way to start building a Charcuterie platter. Using this configuration as my base, this approach makes it effortless to add all the ingredients, and build the composition.

2. The Cheeses
Hard cheese like cheddar or pecorino, and soft cheese like burrata or brie. Arrange cheese wedges in a visually pleasant display, leaving room for the rest of the food categories. Creating an "S" design is the easiest way to compose the cheese on the plate.

3. The Meat
Prosciutto, bresaola, salami, both sliced and whole, and a pâté. First, pile the thinly-sliced prosciutto near a wedge of cheese, then fan the sliced salami folded into a fan pattern next to an olive bowl. Place the whole salami in an open space.

4. The Fruits, Olives, and Nuts
Green and black olives, capers, pickled and stuffed sweet peppers, fresh berries, grapes, fresh figs, and dried fruits. Place the berries, grapes, or figs to fill in holes in your composition board. Olives, grapes, and nuts can all be placed in small bowls.

5. The Jellies, Jams, Spreads, Crackers, and Breads
Jams or jellies in small jars can be placed in a space with a small spoon inserted. Layer crackers lined up and standing in a row into remaining cracks and spaces.

Your shopping list might also include:

Cheeses, both hard cheese like cheddar or pecorino, and soft cheese like burrata or brie

Meats, such as thinly-sliced prosciutto, and bresaola and salami, both sliced and whole

Nuts

Grilled veggies, such as peppers, onions, artichokes, and pickles

Pâté, tapenades, olives

Jellies, sweet and savory jams, and honeycomb

Berries, figs, grapes (green, red, or purple), dates, along with dried fruits such as apricots or apples

Rustic breads such as ciabatta, rye, and country breads, not sliced. (Tip: slice the bread yourself, so it has a rustic look.) Crostini or a baguette, nutty crackers, or focaccia

FRITTATA

Serves 8

Frittata in Italina roughly translates as "fried." That said, a frittata is basically an omelet. The best thing about this cocktail snack is that it can be made ahead and left at room temperature 4 to 6 hours, then cut into bite-sized pieces.

One of the practices I find most amazing about an Italian kitchen is how they repurpose food. I like to include leftover vegetables in the ingredients, which makes it very Italian. This Frittata recipe can be customized by what you have in your refrigerator—be creative!

5 eggs, beaten
¼ cup milk
3 cups spinach, or kale (about ½ cup cooked), steamed and drained
2 tablespoons chopped shallots
1 teaspoon salt
½ teaspoon pepper
1 cup grated Parmesan
Optional: peppers, tomatoes, asparagus, or mushrooms, sliced and pre-cooked to reduce moisture)
3 tablespoons olive oil

Preheat the oven to 350°F.

In a large bowl, combine all the ingredients except the oil.

In a medium cast-iron skillet over medium heat, warm the oil, and add the egg mixture.

Cook 3 minutes, then transfer the skillet to the oven and bake for 20 minutes, until the eggs are firm.

Cut into bite-sized pieces, and serve warm or at room temperature.

MINI MEATBALLS WITH TOMATO DIPPING SAUCE

Serves 8 to 10

½ pound ground beef
3 cloves garlic, minced
¼ red onion, finely diced
½ cup grated Parmesan
3 tablespoons bread crumbs
1 egg
½ teaspoon salt
1 teaspoon chopped fresh rosemary
1 cup olive oil, for frying

Dipping Sauce:
1 (15-ounce) can crushed tomatoes
1 teaspoon dried oregano
1 teaspoon chopped fresh rosemary
1 clove garlic, minced
1 teaspoon salt

In a large bowl combine the beef, garlic, onion, Parmesan, bread-crumbs, egg, salt, and rosemary. Mix by hand until completely combined. Form small 1-inch meatballs, place them on a cookie sheet, cover, and freeze for 1 hour.

While the meatballs are in the freezer, make the tomato sauce. In a medium saucepot over medium heat, stir together the tomatoes, oregano, rosemary, garlic, and salt, and bring to a simmer. Decrease the heat to low and simmer for 1 hour.

To cook the meatballs, heat the oil in a large frying pan over medium heat, until one meatball placed in the oil sizzles. Use a slotted metal spoon to carefully place the meatballs in batches into the hot oil, leaving enough room for them to roll and fry evenly. Fry 5 to 7 minutes, rolling the meatball so that it cooks on all sides until golden brown. Remove with the slotted spoon, and drain on paper towels. Serve warm with toothpicks or small forks, and the tomato dipping sauce in a bowl on the side.

PROSCIUTTO WITH MELON POPS

Serves 6

1 ripe cantaloupe melon, cut in half and seeded
½ pound thinly sliced prosciutto, cut into 1-inch lengths

Tip: Smell the end of your melon—if it smells sweet and melony, it's ripe; if it has no smell, it's not ready yet.

Use a melon baller to scoop out about 25-30 even melon balls. Wrap the melon balls with prosciutto slices around the balls like a belt, and then secure the ball with a skewer placed like a lollipop. Place on a platter. Serve immediately.

GRANDE ROUGE COCKTAIL

Serves 1

1 ½ ounces **Campari**
½ ounce **Grand Marnier**
2 ounces grapefruit juice
1 orange peel, for garnish

Fill a cocktail shaker with ice, and add the Campari, Grand Marnier, and grapefruit juice.

Shake gently, strain into a large coupe or highball glass, and garnish with the orange peel.

MOSCOW MULE

Serves 1

Crushed ice
1 ½ **ounces vodka**
3 **ounces ginger beer**
2 **teaspoons lime juice**
1 **slice lime**

Fill a copper mug or highball glass with crushed ice, and add the vodka and ginger beer.

Gently stir in the lime juice and garnish with a lime slice.

BLUE LAGOON
Serves 1

I must admit, a blue drink puts me off; however, once you get past the Smurf hue, it's a lovely summer cocktail that is sure to make you smile.

1 ounce vodka
1 ounce blue Curacao
2 ounces lemon soda (I like San Pellegrino, or a bitter lemon soda such as the Fever-Tree brand)
1 pineapple slice
1 maraschino cherry

Fill a Collins glass with ice, pour in the vodka and blue Curacao, and stir to combine. Top off with lemon soda, and garnish with a pineapple slice and a cherry.

MILAN

Even though Milan is not on the Riviera, I have included it in this list for several reasons—the foremost being that the city has long influenced aperitivo style. It is the fashion and furniture design capital of the world, so the people-watching is unparalleled. Perhaps more importantly for us, it's also the best place outside the Riviera to enjoy aperitivo. It will come as no surprise that the ritual is said to have originated here. Any bar or hotel in Milan will offer great aperitivo, and there's a mile-long list of the best classics, like the Negroni. Campari was created in Milan. Even though it's not part of the Italian Riviera, don't miss the chance to take a sidetrip and enjoy an original aperitivo in this fabulous city.

In Italy, a bar can mean a place that serves coffee in the morning, sandwiches at lunch, and aperitivo in the evening. More recently in Milan, a stylish innovation has been born: the newest incarnation of aperitivo, called "apero-cena" (apero-dinner). The theory behind apero-cena comes from the fact that the Milanese leave work and head straight to bars to meet friends for an aperitivo. The bars realized that their patrons were spending the entire evening there, so they thought it would be a great idea to set up buffets of more comprehensive nibbles. The bar may charge 10 to 15 Euros for each cocktail, but that price also includes an all-you-can-eat buffet. The idea is, if you're in Milan, a chic apero is in order, so why not make it dinner?

This idea of apero-cena has caught fire all along the Riviera. Since a number of Milanese residents have vacation homes on the Riviera, it's no surprise this new ritual would spread down the Riviera vacation destinations like wildfire.

Some of my favorite spots for aperitivo in Milan are in chic hotels, such as The Bulgari Hotel, or The Bamboo Bar in The Armani Hotel. But sometimes I prefer old school, so I head to Bar Basso, home of the famous Negroni Sbagliato (Negroni "mistake").

The Negroni Sbagliato is said to be the result of a busy bartender mistakenly using sparkling wine instead of gin in a Negroni. When the barman realized the mistake, he wanted to replace the cocktail, but the guest approved of the taste and a new cocktail was born from a happy accident.

Check out the cool district of Brera, full of marvelous aperitivo bars. I especially love Bar Brera.

In the Galleria at the main piazza in Milan located near the Duomo, the famous bar Camparino is the place to enjoy a Campari on the rocks. The bar may seem overcrowded and touristy, but it's a must to visit. Campari has become the international symbol for aperitivo, and this the place Campari was born. In fact, displaying the Campari logo in a bar has become an international symbol to denote that aperitivo is served there. Insider tip: Go to Camparino before lunch to have a Campari. It's quiet and the perfect perch for the fashionable Milanese sport of people-watching.

More recently, Dolce and Gabbana and Martini collaborated in the creation of an ultra-chic hot spot, the Bar Martini, in the heart of the city. Check it out.

All that is chic is Milan and it's one of the best cities to explore all the aperitivo possibilities.

If you drink nowhere else in Italy, Bar Basso is the place to have a cocktail. Order their signature creation: the Sbagliato Negroni.

This page: A perfect martini from Il Bar at the Bulgari Hotel.

Opposite page, at top: The Bamboo Bar at the Armani Hotel. Below, Il Bar at the Bulgari Hotel Bar.

MILANESE RICE SALAD

Serves 8

2 cups water
1 cup uncooked white rice
3 whole eggs
1 pound smoked salmon, cut into small slices
1 tablespoon olive oil
1 teaspoon vinegar
1 teaspoon salt
¼ teaspoon pepper
1 cup tomatoes, diced
1 cup frozen peas, thawed
1 cup fresh cooked corn, or frozen corn kernels, thawed

Bring the water to a boil in a medium saucepan over medium-high heat. Stir in the rice, reduce the heat to low, cover, and simmer 20 minutes. Remove from heat, and set aside to cool.

Place the eggs in a saucepan and add enough cold water to cover them. Bring the water to a boil over medium-high heat, and immediately remove the pan from the heat, cover, and let the eggs stand in hot water for 10 to 12 minutes. When they are cool enough to handle, peel and dice the eggs.

Cut the salmon into bite-size pieces.

In a small bowl, whisk the oil, vinegar, salt, and pepper together until lightly emulsified; set aside.

In a large mixing or serving bowl, toss the tomatoes, peas, and corn together. Add the salmon, diced eggs, and rice, and gently toss again. Cover and refrigerate for at least 1 hour before serving. Toss with dressing to coat just before serving.

BRIOCHE TEA SANDWICHES
WITH CRÈME FRAÎCHE AND SMOKED SALMON
Serves 8

This is a fancy little sandwich to accompany your fancy cocktail. I love super simple bites, and if you're a fan of smoked salmon and cream cheese, you'll love this variation using crème frâiche. This is also a lovely nibble for a brunch aperitivo.

8 small brioche rolls (3 to 4 inches round)
1½ pounds quality smoked salmon, thinly sliced
1 cup crème fraîche
1 cup micro greens, such as arugula or radish greens

Slice each roll in half. Place 2 slices salmon on each bottom half. Top with a dollop of crème fraîche, and garnish with micro greens. Cover with the top of the roll, and secure each sandwich with a toothpick.

SHRIMP SALAD WITH CUCUMBER SLICES
Serves 8

1 pound small shrimp, peeled
2 celery stalks, roughly chopped
1 tablespoon red onion, finely chopped
¼ cup mayonnaise
½ teaspoon salt
2 teaspoons chopped chives
1 large cucumber, sliced into 30 (⅛- inch) rounds

Blanch the shrimp in boiling water for 2 minutes, or until pink. Drain in a colander.

Combine the shrimp, celery, onion, mayonnaise, and salt. Toss gently with the chives.

To serve, you may mound the salad atop the cucumber slices, or arrange the cucumber slices around the salad so that guests can help themselves.

TOKYO SPRITZ

Serves 1

Bamboo Bar—one of my favorite bars in Milan—is located in the Armani Hotel.

Giovanni D'Andolfi is the very creative barman there and always makes the perfect cocktails for Aperitivo. Here are a few of the Armani Bamboo Bar's specialty cocktails. Make sure you ask Giovanni to make you one of these.

2 ounces Aperol
½ teaspoon wasabi paste
½ teaspoon freshly grated ginger
2 ounces chilled prosecco
1 ounce chilled ginger ale
1 orange wedge

Fill a cocktail shaker with ice and add the Aperol, wasabi, and ginger, and shake to combine. Strain into a large glass, top with the chilled prosecco and ginger ale, and garnish with an orange wedge.

MARTINI BALSAMICO

Serves 1

2 ounces gin (I prefer Gin Mare)
½ ounce white balsamic vinegar
4 drops lemon essential oil

Fill a glass shaker with ice and stir in the gin and vinegar until combined.

Strain into a chilled martini glass, add the lemon oil drops, and serve.

MANHATTAN

Serves 1

The Bulgari Hotel, in the busy city center of Milan, is quiet and chic, with a wood-paneled bar room and an oval bar. It's a very popular apero destination during fashion week—a place to see and be seen.

2 ounces bourbon
¾ ounce sweet vermouth
3 dashes Angostura bitters
1 Luxardo brand cherry, to garnish (see Sources, page 234)

Combine all ingredients in cocktail shaker filled with ice. Shake vigorously to chill, then strain into a chilled martini glass. Garnish with a cherry in the glass.

ITALIAN CHERRIES

Amarena cherries have long been adored by Italians and foodies everywhere for their intense cherry flavor, sweetness, and versatility. The word "amarena" refers to a specific variety of dark wild cherry from the Bologna and Modena regions of Italy. The name of the variety is derived from the Italian word for bitter, "amara," and although these cherries are slightly bitter when compared to other varieties, they are preserved in sweet, thick syrup that leaves no hint of bitterness. These cherries often come in beautiful little reusable bottles.

NEGRONI SBAGLIATO SHAKERATO

Serves 1

It's difficult to say something about Bar Basso that has not already been written. It's the most classic Italian bar you will ever set foot in. The owner is famous for this cocktail, and it all started as a mistake—but a happy mistake, and those are the best kind. To me, Bar Basso looks like what a bar should look like: it's messy and un-kept but with a chic décor. It seems immediately authentic and warm and friendly, but still somewhat chaotic. I was surprised when I ordered my first apero and they brought me a small bowl of potato chips—I didn't realize how much a part of apero chips are in Italy. Bar Basso stacks them ten bowls deep and chips are always served with the Bar Basso signature cocktail, the Negroni Sbagliato.

Great-looking people of all ages congregate until late into the night. The blaring neon bar sign is a beacon leading you to cross the street and order a drink here. Settle in and watch the ultimate sartorial scene unfold. It's quintessential Milan.

1 ounce sweet vermouth
1 ounce Campari

1 ounce lightly sparkling wine
1 orange slice

Fill a glass with ice and add the vermouth and Campari. Top with sparkling wine, stir to combine, and garnish with an orange slice.

JAMES BOND "VESPER" MARTINI COCKTAIL

(From the movie *Casinò Royale*)
Serves 1

Lillet blanc is a wine-based aperitif from Podenac, France.

3 ounces gin
1 ounce vodka

½ ounce Lillet blanc
   (see Sources, page 234)
1 twist lemon

Half-fill a cocktail shaker with ice and add the gin, vodka, and Lillet blanc. Shake well, and strain into a chilled martini glass. Garnish with a twist of lemon.

CAMPARI SODA

Serves 1

3 ounces Campari
Splash of soda
1 orange slice

Fill a highball glass with ice, and add the Campari and a splash of soda. Garnish with a slice of orange.

CAMPARI, A SUCCESS STORY

The Galleria Vittrio Emanuele II is located in the center of the city near the duomo, near where Campari was created by Gaspare Campari in 1860. The bright red color of the liquor was originally created with carmine dye, derived from crushed cochineal insects. He opened the Campari Café, now called the Camparino Bar, in the late 1800s in this same area near the duomo, and the café was immensely popular, and is still. Campari was served only in this bar until Gaspare's son thought it was a good idea to distribute it and allow other bars to sell it. To say this idea was a success is an understatement.

Campari umbrellas and signs can be seen in just about every bar in Italy. That's because, under the direction of Davide Campari, Gaspare's son, the company required bars that bought Campari to display the Campari Bitters sign. A bit of brilliant marketing from the early 1900s that's still going strong today.

THE ANGEL WORE RED COCKTAIL

Serves 1

The Martini brand is one of two of the most famous Italian alcohol brands in Italy. I had the pleasure of attending the annual barman competition sponsored by Martini not long ago, and lucky for me the four top barmen were kind enough to share their cocktail recipes for this book. If I had to pick a favorite, it would be Dominic's "The Angel Wore Red."

2 ounces Martini Bianco
1 ounce Martini Bitter, or Campari
½ teaspoon crème de menthe
2½ ounces lager beer
Lemon zest, as garnish

Fill a mixing glass with ice and stir in all of the ingredients. Pour into a tall Collins glass filled with ice (preferably large cubes). Garnish with a heavy sprinkling of lemon zest.

Dominic Whisson, barman at the The Savoy in London, and formidable competitor at the Martini Barman Competition.

L'APERTIVO COCKTAIL
Serves 1

Miguel Perez Munoz, head barman for Solange Cocktail Bar and Luxury Spirits, from Barcelona, has created a cocktail with the flair of a bullfighter in the ring. Watching him present his cocktail for the competition was as exciting as the cocktail itself.

2 ounces Martini Rosso
1 ounce Martini Bitter, or Campari
1 ounce gin
½ ounce Curaçao
2 ounces sage simple syrup (recipe below)

Mix all the ingredients in a cocktail shaker and pour into a highball glass half-filled with ice.

Sage Simple Syrup
Serves 4

1 cup water
1 cup sugar
5 sage leaves

Bring all ingredients to a simmer in a small saucepan over medium heat, and cook for 10 minutes, stirring occasionally. Remove from the heat, allow to cool, then strain into a lidded jar or container. This syrup will keep, sealed and refrigerated, for 2 weeks.

MILANO TORINO
Serves 1

2 ounces Campari
2 ounces vermouth
1 slice orange

Fill a highball glass with ice and add the Campari and vermouth. Stir, and garnish with an orange slice.

UN AMERICANO A TORINO

Serves 1

"The Americano, besides being one of the best-known drinks in the world, is a word that we find in many places, and in many titles. It's a word that makes us dream." As barman Walter Gosso tells it, the inspiration for his cocktail came to him from the film An American in Paris. *He named his cocktail "An American in Torino," a nod to the screen classic.*

2 ounces Martini Rosato
2 ounces Martini Bitter, or Campari
2 dashes Fee Brothers Plum Bitters
4 ounces Chinotto
Squeeze of lemon
1 orange peel

Fill a Collins glass with ice and add the Martini Rosato, Martini Bitter, and the Plum Bitter. Top with Chinotto, and a squeeze of lemon over the top, then garnish with the orange peel.

POPOLO COCKTAIL

Serves 1

This cocktail was presented by the barman from Hotel Les Bains in Paris, Nicolas Lasjuiriallas.

1½ ounces Martini Bianco
1 ounce Kina
3 drops Schnapps
1 lemon wedge
4 ounces tonic water
1 grapefruit wedge

Fill a balloon glass with ice and stir to chill the glass. Pour in the Martini Bianco, then the Kina, Schnapps, and finish with a squeeze of lemon. Stir, and add the tonic water. Garnish with a grapefruit wedge.

LIST OF BARS AND HOTELS BY CITY

Bars:

Bordighera:
La Reserve, Via Arziglia, 20, 18012 Bordighera IM, Italy
www.ristorantelareserve.com
La Casa del Caffè, 13 Corso Italia Bordighera IM, Italy
Buga Buga, 13 Corso Italia -Bordighera IM, Italy
www.ristorantebugabuga.com/chi-siamo.html

San Remo:
Vino e Panino, Corso Augusto Mombello, 56, 18038 Sanremo IM, Italy
tel. +39 0184 524290
Morgana Victory, Lungomare Trento e Trieste, 16, 18038 Sanremo IM, Italy
Tel. +39 0184 591620

Imperia:

Portici della banchina di Oneglia
Braceria Matama, Calata Gian Battista Cuneo 13, Molo Corto, 18100 Imperia, Province of Imperia, Italy
Damare, 37, Calata Gian Battista Cuneo 18100 Imperia IM, Italy
tel. 0183 880083
Canna Ramella, 53, Calata Gian Battista Cuneo-18100 Imperia IM
Bar La Conchuglia, Via G.b. Cuneo , 5 18100 IMPERIA IM, Italy
tel. 0183 767761

Alassio:
Café Roma, Corso Dante Alighieri, 312-17021 Alassio, SV, Italy
Café Mozart, Passaggio Italia 3, 17021 Alassio SV, Italy
La Cambusa, Passeggiata Cadorna, 12, 17021 Alassio SV, Italy
Baba Beach, www.bababeachalassio.com/

La Laterna, www.facebook.com/
lalanternaalassio/?rf=388493144531981
Via Milano 5 Alassio 17021
San Lorenzo, Via Vittorio Veneto 69, 17021 Alassio—tel. +39
0182 640601
Clapsy Restaurant, www.clapsy.it/ Passeggiata D. Grollero 18
17021 Alassio SV, Italy—tel. +39 - 0182/660573

Loano:
YCML Club Molo Centrale, Banchina Porto 17025 Loano SV, Italy —
tel. +39 019 667835, Fax +39 019 6779805
www.ycml.it/en/explore/layout/club/the-ycml.html

Genova:
Cavo Via di Fossatello, 35-37RR, Genova, Italy—tel. +39 010 209 1226
www.cavo.it/
Cambi Café, Vico Falamonica, 1r 16123 Genova, Italy - cambicafe.
com/contatti.html
Les Rouges, Piazza Campetto, 8, 16123 Genova, Italy www.
lesrouges.it/
Café Degli Specchi, Salita Pollaiuoli 43, 16123, Genova, Italy www.
facebook.com/caffedeglispecchigenova
Bar Berto, Piazza dell'Erbe, 6, 16123 Genova, Italy
La Strambata, Piazza Nettuno 5R, Boccadasse, Genova, Italy
Antica Trattoria Dindi, Piazzetta Nettuno Genova (Boccadasse),
Italy - www.dindiboccadasse.it/ristorante/
Bar Mangini, Piazza Corvetto 3r; 16122 Genova, Italy—tel. +39
010 564013

Santa Margherita:
Grand Hotel Miramare, www.grandhotelmiramare.it/en/
Via Milite Ignoto 30 16038 Santa Margherita Ligure / ITALY
tel. +39 0185 287013
Bar Piero, Via V. Veneto, 6, 16038 Santa Margherita Ligure GE, Italy
tel. +39 0185 287514
Bar Black Stallion, Piazza Vittorio Veneto, 22, 16038 Santa
Margherita Ligure GE, Italy

Il Fiocco American Bar, Via Gramsci, 16038 Santa Margherita Ligure GE, Italy

tel.: +39 0185 280150

Da Nello, Via A. Gramsci, 105, 16038 Santa Margherita Ligure GE, Italy

tel.:+39 0185 286505

Paraggi Beach Clubs, https://en.wikipedia.org/wiki/Paraggi

Portofino:

La Gritta, Calata Marconi, 20, 16034 Portofino GE, Italy

tel. +39 0185 269126

Bar Mariuccia, Piazza Martiri dell'Olivetta, 27, 16034 Portofino GE, Italy

tel. +39 0185 269080

Hotel Splendido, Salita Baratta, 16, 16034 Portofino GE, Italy

tel. +39 0185 267801

Hotel Piccolo, Via Duca degli Abruzzi, 31, 16034 Portofino GE, Italy

tel. +39 0185 269015

Levanto:

Bar Casino, Piazza Colombo, 19015 Levanto, Italy

tel. +39 349 844 842

Bar Nadia, Passeggiata a Mare, 19015 Levanto Italy

Piper Bar, Arenile Rio Gavazzo, 19015 Levanto SP, Italy

Tel. +39 339 416 6098

Portovenere:

La Vigna Di Nettuno, Calata Doria, 19025 Portovenere SP, Italy

tel. +39 0187 791775

Locanda Lorena, Via Cavour, 4, 19025 Isola Palmaria SP, Italy

tel. +39 0187 792370 www.locandalorena.com/

Lerici:

Bar Corona, Via Amerigo, Lerici, Italy

Phone +39 0187 967556

Bar Il Pontile, Via Lungomare Vassallo, Lerici, SP 19032, Italy

tel. +39 0187 968609

Eco del Mare, Strada Lerici - Tellaro
Località Maramozza n° 4 Lerici 19032 (SP) Italy tel. +39 0187 966863
www.ecodelmare.it

Milano:
Ceresio 7, Via Ceresio, 7, 20154 Milano, Italy
tel.+39 02 3103 9221
Copacabana Temakeria, Via Cesare Cesariano, 14,
20154 Milano, Italy
tel. +39 02 8905 9867
Grand Hotel Milan, Via Alessandro Manzoni, 29,
20121 Milano, Italy
tel. +39 02 723141 www.grandhoteletdemilan.it
Hotel Bulgari, Via Privata Fratelli Gabba, 7b, 20121 Milano, Italy
tel. +39 02 805 8051 www.bulgarihotels.com/en_US/milan
Bamboo Bar Armani Hotel Bar, Via Alessandro Manzoni, 31,
20121 Milano, Italy
tel. +39 02 8883 8888
www.milan.armanihotels.com/dine/dine_armani_lounge_en.html
Bar Basso, via Plinio 39, Milano tel. +39 02 2940 0580
http://barbasso.com/main
Camparino Bar, Galleria Vittorio Emanuele angolo
Piazza Duomo - Milano
tel. +39 02 86464435 www.camparino.it/
H Club Diana, Viale Piave 42, Milan tel. +39 220 582 004 www.
hclub-diana.com
Bar Brera, Via Brera 23 20121 Milan tel. +39 02 877091
Bar Martini, Corso Venezia 15, 20122 Milan tel. +390276011154
http://www.dolcegabbana.com/martini/
Terrazza Martini, Piazza Armando Diaz 7 20122 Milan tel. +39
0119419811
www.martinierossi.it/terrazze/milano/default.aspx
Il Bar at Rinascente, The perfect view of the Duomo, from the
famous department store roof bar- 7th Floor - Food Hall tel.
+39 02 46771.1 la Rinascente S.p.A via washington, 7020146
milanohttps://www.rinascente.it/rinascente/en/barcafe/11796

RECIPE INDEX

SOURCES

Liquor:
Cynar: www.craftspiritsxchange.com
Suze: www.craftspiritsxchange.com
Lillet Blanc: https://www.reservebar.com/lillet-blanc

Food:
Taggiasca Olives: www.oliviersandco.com/pantry
Bottarga: www.buonitalia.com
Lemon Sugar: www.amazon.com/lemn-cocktail-sugar-drink-rimmer
Luxardo Cherries: https://www.williams-sonoma.com/products/
luxardo-maraschino-cherries
Sundried Tomatoes: Whole Foods
Italian Canned Tuna: Whole Foods
Roland Anchovies: https://www.amazon.com/gp/product/
B001GVIUDQ/
Edible Spoons: https://www.amazon.com/Bocado-Edible-Spoon-24-Pk/
dp/B074LWQ662

ACKNOWLEDGMENTS

I have so many people to thank: first and foremost my husband Frank who's an amazing support and a wonderful photographer and teacher. He's been there to photograph and edit, and he taught me how to use my camera. Mostly, I want to thank him for cheering me on every step of the way. He's definitely my favorite drinking partner of all time. I raise my glass to you Frank, I love you.

Grazie mille, to my best friend and Italian drinking buddy, Forrest. You are a gentleman and a scholar, but mostly you drink like no other, and without you I would truly be lost in Italy. You have shown me the secrets that Italy holds, and for that I am forever grateful.

Oma, a cocktail connoisseur and my best friend, my sister, we have toasted to many life events together, and having you in Italy with me is always a joy! You've taught me a lot about life, love, and friendship—and, of course, drinking.

To my incredible staff: Kayla, Justin, Rachel, Megan, Hannah, Glenn, all of you who schlepped, lugged, and helped me style and photograph this book, I am forever grateful. This was the best job ever—driving on the Italian coastline, ordering loads of drinks, photographing them, and then all of you drinking them so that I was the designated driver. You should have paid me . . . hahaha.

Thanks to photographer Deborah Whitlaw Llewellyn for filling in the blanks on the food and cocktail recipe shots; and to the incredible Janice Shay, my guru and spirit animal, the best editor/book packager ever. Your wise words and guidance through this process always humbled me.

Grazie, Penny, you were the first creative director I've ever met, and have been a creative inspiration ever since—thank you for your beautiful map illustration. Your talent blows me away, and you always have a kind word—you're such an elegant lady.

Thanks to the barmen and bar owners all around Italy who shared their recipes with me. Grazie to Martini for opening their factory doors in Turin; and to Giorgio, day-drinking in the Martini headquarters bar was always a treat.

Leo and Elizabeth, thank you for showing me all the best drinking spots in Alassio, you are the best friends to apero with; and to Monica for being a lively part of my aperitivo experiences in Alassio and St. Tropez.

Thank you to my children, Alex and Levi, who are now of legal drinking age and always show me a thing or two about enjoying a modern new cocktail. They are a part of my continuing education. I love you both.

This book could not have been completed without the many people that I cherish, respect, and am honored to call friends and colleagues. Cheers until our next aperitivo!

STANDARD CONVERSIONS

METRIC AND IMPERIAL CONVERSIONS
(These conversions are rounded for convenience)

Ingredient	Cups/ Tablespoons/ Teaspoons	Ounces	Grams/ Milliliters
Fruit, dried	1 cup	4 ounces	120 grams
Fruits or veggies, chopped	1 cup	5 to 7 ounces	145 to 200 grams
Fruits or veggies, pureed	1 cup	8.5 ounces	245 grams
Honey, maple syrup, or corn syrup	1 tablespoon	0.75 ounce	20 grams
Liquids: cream, milk, water, or juice	1 cup	8 fluid ounces	240 milliliters
Salt	1 teaspoon	0.2 ounces	6 grams
Spices: cinnamon, cloves, ginger, or nutmeg (ground)	1 teaspoon	0.2 ounce	5 milliliters
Sugar, brown, firmly packed	1 cup	7 ounces	200 grams
Sugar, white	1 cup/ 1 tablespoon	7 ounces/0.5 ounce	200 grams/12.5 grams
Vanilla extract	1 teaspoon	0.2 ounce	4 grams

Liquids

8 fluid ounces = 1 cup = ½ pint
16 fluid ounces = 2 cups = 1 pint
32 fluid ounces = 4 cups = 1 quart
128 fluid ounces = 16 cups = 1 gallon